HOLLYWOOD FIRE-RESCUE & BEACH SAFETY DEPARTMENT

Turner®
Publishing Company

Nashville, Tennessee • Paducah, Kentucky

TURNER PUBLISHING COMPANY

200 4th Avenue North • Suite 950
Nashville, Tennessee 37219
(615) 255-2665

412 Broadway • P.O. Box 3101
Paducah, Kentucky 42002-3101
(270) 443-0121

www.turnerpublishing.com

Copyright 2008: Hollywood Fire Department
Publishing Rights: Turner Publishing Company

ISBN-13: 978-1-68162-193-7
Library of Congress Control Number: 2008928232

0 9 8 7 6 5 4 3 2 1

City Commission 4

Letter from the Chief 6

Fire Chief's History 8

Department History 11

Administration 20

Support Services.. 26

Fire Marshal's Office 43

Explorer Post 1375 48

Employee of the Year 52

Firefighter of the Year 53

Operations 56

Photo Gallery 85

Local 1375 145

Pension Fund 147

HFRA 148

Benevolent 151

Last Alarm 153

September 11, 2001 154

Yearbook Committee 157

Acknowledgments.................................... 159

.... 166

Firefighters Joe Eutsey and Scott Bazy on the hose.

The City Commission is the legislative body that governs the City and has a fiduciary responsibility to the citizens. As set by the City Charter, the Mayor and six Commissioners are elected every four years. Commissioners are elected by single-member districts and the Mayor is elected at-large. The City of Hollywood Commission consists of Peter Bober, Mayor; Frances Russo, Vice Mayor representing District 5; Patty Asseff, District 1; Beam Furr, District 2; Heidi O'Sheehan, District 3; Richard S. Blattner, District 4; and Linda Sherwood, District 6.

A City Manager and City Attorney are appointed by the City Commission to oversee the day-to-day operations. The City Manager carries out the policies made by the Commission, prepares the annual budget and directs and coordinates all City departments. Cameron D. Benson was appointed as the City Manager in June 2002. The City Attorney oversees all legal matters of city government including drafting ordinances, writing contracts, managing litigation and developing legal opinions.

Peter Bober, Mayor

Frances Russo, Vice Mayor
Representing District 5

Patty Asseff, District 1

Beam Furr, District 2

Heidi O'Sheehan, District 3

Richard S. Blattner, District 4

Linda Sherwood, District 6

Cameron D. Benson, City Manager

HOLLYWOOD FIRE / RESCUE AND BEACH SAFETY DEPARTMENT

City of Hollywood, Florida

Office of
Virgil Fernandez
Fire Chief

2741 Stirling Road
Hollywood, Florida 33312-6505
Phone: (954)967-4248 Fax: (954)967-4253)

ISO CLASS ONE DEPARTMENT

Dear Members of Hollywood Fire/Rescue and Beach Safety:

The Hollywood Fire Department was formed in 1924 and was comprised of 19 men and 2 pieces of fire apparatus. Since then, the Department has undergone many changes. In 1987, the Department's name was changed to Hollywood Fire Rescue, and then in 1996, the name was changed again; this time to Hollywood Fire/Rescue and Beach Safety.

That last name change reflects how we have gone from almost an exclusive fire suppression department, to a full service fire rescue and beach safety department providing not only fire suppression but emergency medical services and special operations, to include hazardous materials responses, technical rescue team, dive rescue, beach safety, fire inspection and investigation and public education as well as many other services that have a direct impact on the quality of life and safety within the City of Hollywood.

The department has evolved to its present size of almost 300 personnel of which 223 are sworn firefighters. The department's ISO rating went from a class 4 to a rating of class 2 in 1999 and then in 2001 the department was rated a Class 1 Fire Department. Less than 1% of all departments in the country receive a class 1 rating which reflects our commitment to service and excellence.

Hollywood has always been a progressive department and a leader in the fire service. In 2005, a general obligation bond was passed by over 70% of the voters in order to reconstruct 3 of the existing fire rescue stations and to build a new fire station, training facility and maintenance facility as well as to purchase an aerial, engine and an Advance Life Support Rescue.

By the time this book is published, the Hollywood Firefighters will respond to nearly 28,000 alarms per year. The one thing that has stayed constant from the early beginnings until today is the need for people to deliver the service. These pages are filled with those people who have given their lives and dedicated them selves to protecting others. This book is a tribute to that dedication. I am truly honored to be a member of the Hollywood Fire Rescue and Beach Safety family.

Proudly,

Virgil Fernandez, Fire Chief

Virgil Fernandez, Fire Chief

Since the inception of the Department, there have been thirteen individuals to hold the position of Fire Chief.

In 1924, the Hollywood Fire Department was organized by private investors and R. N. Hershey was appointed as the first Fire Chief of the City of Hollywood Fire Department. He previously held the position of Fire Chief of the Lake Worth Fire Department. When the City incorporated one year later they named Hershey the city's first municipal fire chief.

R. N. Hershey

In May, 1929, serving in the dual role of Fire Chief and City Manager, C. E. Burgoon replaced Chief Hershey. Fifteen months later he relinquished his position as Fire Chief to another "dual-role" chief but with a slight variation.

No Photo Available for C. E. Burgoon

A. M. Wittkamp would then serve as both the fire and police chiefs for the next six years.

A. M. Whittkamp

In July, 1936, A. J. Wilkie began his six year tenure and is remembered for his community service work, including the construction and dedication of the Fireman's Community House in 1940.

A. J. Wilkie

The most historic span of any chief began on August 3 1942, with the appointment of Holloway Lee Cook. An origina member of the department, he actually resided with his family at the old Polk Street fire station. He served as fire chief unti his retirement in September, 1968. Upon his retirement, Chie Cook had served as a member of the department for over 4C years.

Holloway Cook

When Chief Cook retired, John Gerkin served as fire chief for just less than three years. At his request, he returned to the rank of captain and was re-assigned to the Fire Marshal's office.

John Gerkin

Chief Gerkin's successor in May, 1971, was John Coyne; first as "acting" then as the permanent Chief. Coyne, the first president of the firefighters union, remains the only person to have held the top position on both sides of the labor and management relationship. He served over nine years before retiring in 1980.

John Coyne

Ed Race, Chief Coyne's assistant chief (now known as deputy chief), was promoted to the rank of Fire Chief in August, 1980. Chief Race served approximately twenty-two months prior to retirement.

Ed Race

In June, 1982, Jim Ward was promoted to Fire Chief from his position as Rescue Division Chief (now known as the Division Chief of Support Services). With his retirement on October 1, 1994, Chief Ward's 12 years as chief leaves him as the second longest serving fire chief in the history of the department.

Jim Ward

On November 28, 1994, after a national search, Herminio Lorenzo became the next fire chief and only the second to be hired from outside the department. He was the Chief of the the City of Hialeah Fire Department prior to his appointment. Chief Lorenzo would serve until February 15, 1999. The illustrious career of Chief Lorenzo continued as he became the Fire Chief of Broward County Fire Rescue and currently serves as the Fire Chief for the Miami-Dade Fire Rescue Department.

Herminio Lorenzo

Division Chief Randall Burrough would then replace Chief Lorenzo on March 22, 1999. As fire chief, Chief Burrough was instrumental in the completion of the "new" Fire Station 74. During his service as Fire Chief, Chief Burrough also oversaw the Department attaining an Insurance Services Offices (ISO) Class 1 rating. Chief Burrough retired on September 27, 2002.

Randall Burrough

After a nationwide search for a new chief, Deputy Chief Edward Moran would be promoted to the rank of fire chief on July 22, 2003. Chief Moran, who had worked his way up through the ranks of the Department, would serve as Fire Chief for eighteen months before retiring on January 21, 2005. He is currently serving as the Fire Chief for the Town of Palm Beach, Florida.

Edward Moran

Another nationwide search would find our current Fire Chief, Virgil Fernandez who joined the Department after 23 years of service with the City of Miami Fire Department. Chief Fernandez progressed through the ranks last serving as the Fire Marshal during the City of Miami's economic development. Chief Fernandez is also a Task Force Leader with the Urban Search and Rescue Team and responded to assist with the post 9/11 recovery efforts. He began his tenure with the Department on June 1, 2005.

Virgil Fernandez

From a privately owned, one station, single engine company operation in 1924, to the six station, multi-discipline, municipal fire rescue service of today, The Hollywood Fire Rescue and Beach Safety Department is proud of its heritage and place in the history of the fire service.

The City of Hollywood Fire Rescue and Beach Safety Department was first organized in 1924 as a private enterprise and officially became part of the City in 1926.

The following is a chronological history of the formation and Hollywood Fire Department.

Fall 1921 - Plans are developed and Hollywood's first lot is staked out at the corner of what is now Hollywood Boulevard and 21st Avenue. Indianapolis, Indiana, inspires the idea of a broad, central boulevard with several circle parks intersecting it. Long Beach, California, inspires strict building codes, zoning and development; Hollywood, California inspires the name.

1924 - The Hollywood Land & Water Company, owned by city founder Joseph W. Young, organizes its own private fire department. One fire engine is purchased and R. N. Hershey is hired as Fire Chief.

November 25, 1925 - The City of Hollywood is incorporated, but continues under the protection of a private fire department.

January 15, 1926 - The Hollywood Land & Water Company turns its fire protection services over to the new municipality and the City of Hollywood Fire Department is officially born. R. N. Hershey is retained as its Fire Chief.

September 18, 1926 - The City is struck by a devastating hurricane.

March 1929 - C. E. Burgoon begins a five-month tenure as both City Manager and Fire Chief.

August 30, 1929 - A. M. Wittkamp is assigned to the dual positions of both Police and Fire chief.

Autumn 1932 - Desperately attempting to recover from a depression era and post-hurricane financial crunch, the City authorizes the issuance of scrip, in lieu of cash, in order to pay municipal employees, including firefighters.

July 23, 1936 - A. J. Wilkie is named as the new Fire Chief.

Spring 1937 - Fire Department personnel become part of the Civil Service Act.

Spring 1940 - The "Fireman's Community House" is dedicated.

July 21, 1940 - The Department suffers its first line-of-duty death when firefighter Gilbert J. Higgins is electrocuted by falling into high-voltage wires at the Great Southern Hotel fire.

August 3, 1942 - Holloway L. Cook is appointed to Fire Chief.

October 16, 1947 - The area is still recovering from the September 17th hurricane when a second hurricane strikes on October 11th. Severe flooding prompts the City of Dania to carve a 40' x 400' channel ("the Dania Cut-Off Canal") to drain flood waters into the inter-coastal waterway.

November 10, 1951 - Driver Engineer James F. Woodruff dies while fighting a fire at the Great Southern Hotel.

April 12, 1952 - While attempting an ocean rescue, Driver Engineer Jay Holland drowns on Hollywood Beach in front of the Surf Hotel.

January 5, 1959 - A dropped cigarette is believed to have ignited a fire that destroys one wing of the Riverside Military Academy, prompting the construction of an entirely new complex.

July 1, 1960 - The Hollywood Professional Fire Fighters are chartered as Local # 1375 of the International Association of Fire Fighters.

August 1960 – Firefighters begin a program of courtesy house-to-house fire inspections that includes offering highly reflective stickers for handicapped residents who may need immediate or special assistance during an emergency.

January 24, 1961 - In a potentially historic public hearing, the Hollywood City Commission resists public and editorial pressures and declines to merge the police and fire departments into a single public safety department.

Thanksgiving Day, 1962 - The Hollywood Fire Department Rescue Squad is officially placed in operation. Firefighters William Clark and Edward Race respond to an auto accident at Arthur Street and North 29th Avenue. The squads only provided first aid and transport to the emergency room, if necessary.

January 1963 - The Hollywood Professional Building fire threatens the entire downtown area and causes $80,000 in damages.

January 15, 1964 - The Florida State Theater is destroyed by an early morning fire.

December 1, 1964 – Fire Station #3 at 3401 Hollywood Boulevard is assigned first alarm responsibilities when Hollywood annexes areas to the west and, overnight, the city's geographical boundaries are increased by approximately 2,700 homes and 7,700 residents.

January 1965 - City officials dedicate new Fire Station #4 located at 1810 North 64th Avenue. The station serviced the newly annexed area that was formerly "West Hollywood".

PARTICIPATE IN DEDICATION — Mayor William Zinkil, extreme left, was featured speaker at the official dedication of the new Fire Station #4, 1810 N.W. 64th Ave. The dedication also featured a first-aid demonstration, a tour of the new facility and a look at new fire equipment to be used in the building. The new fire station will service the recently annexed areas in what was formerly West Hollywood. Also participating in the ceremonies were from left, foreground, City Commissioner B. L. David, Arnold Toguzzi, representing Togzoli Brothers, contractors for the structure; City Commissioner David Keating and Arthur Frimet, architect for the new city facility. Mrs. Opal Mills, president of the Driftwood Home Owners Association, presided at the refreshment table, which was manned by members of the Association. The Driftwood Aerot Junior High School Band provided music for the occasion and "Miss Flame," Linda Heuring of McArthur High School, cut the ceremonial ribbon to mark the official opening.

1966 - The Department's "Rescue Squad", driven by Firefighter Martin Hodos, is struck by another vehicle and overturns while responding to an emergency call. No one is seriously injured from the accident.

September 7, 1966 - Lieutenant Evo Frattini directs a thirty-hour dive training course which was successfully completed by twenty members of the department, and became the largest professional underwater search and recovery squad in Florida.

October 1967 - In a proud moment for the department, Lt. Evo Frattini receives the Broward Williams Fireman of the Year Award in a ceremony held in Tallahassee.

1968 - Chief Holloway Lee Cook announces his retirement after forty-three years of service to the Fire Department; his last twenty-seven as Chief.

August 30, 1968 - Fire destroys the Hollywood Central Elementary School.

March 20, 1970 - Lt. Joseph Mello receives the eighth annual Distinguished Service Award sponsored by the Jewish War Veterans, Post 613.

April 12, 1970 - After 43 years of service, the Department closes the main station at 19th Avenue and Polk Street and moves the district's operations to 421 North 21st Avenue. The old station's four traditional brass poles are removed and sold to a northern fire department.

September 1971 - A fire at Family Furniture Store gains devastating headway following a twenty-six minute delay in reporting the alarm to the HFD. The blaze went on to be the worst fire of the year.

THIS YEAR'S LARGEST BLAZE — Losses from a Sunday night fire at the block-long Family Furniture store, 1616 S. State Road 7, in Hollywood will run from $100,000 to $130,000, Assistant Fire Chief W. N. Campbell said today, making it the biggest fire this year to date here. The blaze gutted this entire south half of the store, while the other half had smoke and water damage. Fire prevention bureau officials said the fire started from a fluorescent light which was in a bedroom furniture display. Quick action by firemen "contained" the fire but it had been going on for some time before they arrived at 9:42 p.m. The roof was about to cave in and steel girders were melting in the 1,000-degree blaze, Campbell said. No one was injured. The store was closed when the fire started.

January 10, 1972 - After the Hollywood Fire Department cites severe fire safety hazards; the *Queen Elizabeth* sails away, catches fire and capsizes.

June 28, 1972 - A high-pressure gas line breaks and ignites a thirty-minute series of explosions in the acetylene storage room at Liquid Carbonics Corporation.

Firefighters Continue to Douse Plant to Prevent More Explosions

July 30, 1972 – The Driftwood Recreation Center sustains an estimated $200,000 in damages after a suspicious fire destroys its interior. An area teenager is later convicted of arson.

October 2, 1972 – The Department's first African American firefighters are sworn in. They are: Ernest Evans, Sherrick Thomas, and Lonnie James.

THEY'RE THE FIRST — Sworn in this morning were Hollywood's first black firemen. From left are Ernest C. Evans, 714 NW Sixth St., Hallandale; Sherrick Thomas, 4413 SW 20th St., West Hollywood, and Lonnie James Jr., 31 NW Tenth Ct, Dania. All three men have satisfactorily completed 240 hours of the minimum standard training program and were assigned today to regular shift.

July 10, 1973 – Fire from a discarded cigarette destroys the bed area of the Diplomat Hotel guest room of Frank Fontaine, who starred as "Crazy Guggenheim" on television's "The Jackie Gleason Show."

August 16, 1973 – The mother of an 11 year old drowning victim drives a rescue van to the hospital so that the two-man crew could perform life-saving CPR. The efforts are successful and dramatize the need for three-man crews. She later jokes "I wonder what people thought seeing the rescue truck being driven by this person in a yellow terrycloth robe?"

December 20, 1974 – Local #1375 sponsors a benefit performance of "The Towering Inferno" at the Hollywood Cinema. Proceeds benefit the drug intervention programs a The Starting Place.

The Towering Ladder

Hollywood's fire fighters were out, equipment and all, to help promote the benefit premiere of "The Towering Inferno" for the Starting Place Thursday night. The hook and ladder truck towered over Young Circle. A rescue vehicle also was at the scene for public viewing. Additional pictures on the benefit are on Page 1C.

Sun-Tattler Photo By John Ashcraft Jr.

February 8, 1975 – Maintenance workers using a blow torch to remove old paint ignite a fire that threatens the original home of Joseph Young. Prompt fire department action saves the historical structure.

February 26, 1975 – President Gerald Ford is a guest at the Diplomat Hotel when a faulty thermostat ignites a fire in the sauna room. A member of the presidential party smells smoke and is credited with detecting the blaze.

Mother Of Accident Victi

By CLARENCE LEINO
Sun-Tattler Staff Writer

A mother who drove a Hollywood Rescue Squad to Memorial Hospital while the two crew members worked in the rear of the van to save her son's life dramatically pointed up the need for a three-man rescue crew.

The South Broward Hospital District Board Tuesday night voted to allocate $184,000 for a district mobile medical service with sophisticated communications between rescue squads and the hospital — and a three-man paramedic trained crew.

Assistant Fire Chief Edward Race said that if the city commission approves his department's budget requests, this will add 18 rescue personnel.

"THE KEY words are 'paramedic trained' and when the equipment is installed at the hospital and in the rescue squads, we will have all the men trained to operate this. Right now 12 out of our 44 men have completed paramedic training, which is about a 60-hour course over and above the two-phase emergency medical training that all members have taken." said Race.

Mrs. Morse Johns, of 3816 Adams St., Sunday afternoon ended up driving the rescue squad to the hospital when the vehicle was transporting her 11-year-old son after he had been pulled from the family pool.

Her son, Mark, has a history of epilepsy and although he is a good swimmer, he had a seizure and went under. A neighbor ran over and gave artificial respiration until the rescue squad arrived.

★ ★ ★

ON THE way to the hospital, Mark stopped breathing and rescue squad men George Fox and Richard Russell both jumped in the rear of the van to work on the boy. Mrs. Johns, who had gone along in the rescue squad, asked if she couldn't drive the van to the hospital.

"The rescue men told her to go ahead, but to drive slow and observe all traffic lights." said Race. "It takes two men in the rear in a case like this, one to apply heart massage and the other to give mouth-to-mouth resuscitation."

Mark was breathing when they reached Memorial later was transferred Broward General Center. He came h day — and is fine.

★ ★ ★

"THE RESCUE are fantastic. I hope the three-men crew like to have. I don't where we were to drive. The rescue power steering and hard to drive." Johns.

Race said the stopped on 35th Jackson Street, a blocks from the J and about a mile fro pital.

He said their munications equip other specialized un

FIREMEN WORK ON FIRE IN HOME BUILT BY JOSEPH YOUNG
Famous Landmark Was Not Seriously Damaged

April 5, 1975 – In classic fire department fashion, Department members "protect their own" by raising funds in support of rookie firefighter William Podger, who lost his home and possessions to a mobile home fire.

July 1975 – The Department is issued drug kits by Dr. Richard Dellerson, Chief of Memorial Hospital's Emergency Room, and becomes the first city in South Broward to implement the Mobile Emergency Service Program (MEMS). Using IV therapy, EKGs, and large orange biophones, medics complete the conversion to an ALS provider system. (MEMS)

April 16, 1976 – 175 municipal employees are sent home on paid leave after a service box fire cuts off electrical power to Hollywood City Hall. In a humorous decision, top city administrators remain in the building and, symbolically, continue to work in the dark.

October 1976 – Portions of the City's old sewer plant are renovated and become the Hollywood Fire College; a facility that can simulate anything from an oil tank explosion to a fire in a ship's hold. Division Chief Warren calls it "a fire instructor's dream come true."

November 17, 1977 – A traditional fire fighter's funeral procession is used to pay final respects to Rescue Division Chief Joseph Mello after his twenty-three years of service.

FIRE CHIEF JOHN COYNE (LEFT) INAUGURATES PARAMEDIC PROGRAM
With Lt. Steve Cuthbert in Rescue Van, Dr. Richard Dellerson Of Memorial

December 1977 – After allegedly calling in sick five minutes too late, George Fox proves that no two department clocks are synchronized and that some deviate from Greenwich Mean Time by as much as eight minutes. In the process, he spends $425 in legal fees to successfully reverse a four-hour ($28) suspension.

August 13, 1978 – The first major Diplomat Hotel fire occurs.

May 21, 1979 – Fire damages the "Scheherazade Room" at the Diplomat Hotel. The second floor banquet room sustains $25,000 in losses.

lad To Drive Rescue Van

in the rescue squads e hospital, the trained medics can radio vital of a subject directly into ergency room.

★ ★ ★
EY CAN RADIO heart pulse and breathing plus description of in- to the doctor in the ency room, who can ad- the scene treatment. it is not best to iately transport a per- the hospital, but to ze the patient's condi- Race said.

said it would take two o operate the equipment a third man drove the e squad. However, the r also will be a medic, he added.

e said the large number

of calls by the city's five rescue squads and the type of emer- gencies pointed up the need for the mobile emergency medical service (MEMS).

★ ★ ★
"IN JULY we had 40 heart attack runs, 70 auto accidents and 250 miscellaneous," Race said.

In June it was 39 heart, 69 auto, 224 miscellaneous. In May, 62-75-222; in March, 72,104 and 281; in February, 115,64 and 238. Race noted that the 115 heart attacks in February reflected the increased number of elderly winter residents and visitors.

Race said that the whole budget increase package of the fire department now in the city commission hands was $340,000, but he hoped the hos-

pital board would provide some of the MEMS equipment and lower this figure.

★ ★ ★
HE SAID there may have to be a fee schedule instituted so the patients transported in the MEMS program could con- tribute to the upkeep.

Race noted that the rescue squad does not now transport patients except in extreme emergencies such as with the Johns boy on Sunday. Private ambulances generally are called to transport patients, for which the patient pays.

In the MEMS program, the rescue vehicles necessarily transport many patients because they will be carrying the specialized equipment need to provide enroute treat-

ment, he added.

★ ★ ★
THE HOSPITAL board Tuesday night suggested that a $30 a call charge be made to persons served by the MEMS program, which would about equal a private ambulance transportation charge not in volving oxygen.

Race said that rescue squad personnel currently receive their paramedic training a Mt. Sinai Hospital in Miami He expected this would even tually be provided a Memorial because doctor there also would have to be trained in the use of the telemetry equipment an other procedures in the MEMS system.

June 27, 1980 - Following a burglary at old Station #5 on 56th Avenue, the Department is forced to re-instate a "lock the doors before you respond" policy.

July 5, 1980 - Stating that he's "Still for the fire department", retired Fire Chief John Coyne returns to the labor side of the bargaining table as business agent for the fire fighter's union that he organized twenty years prior.

September 16, 1980 - Eighty fire fighters march along Dixie Highway as they return to work following a three day sickout resulting from stalled contract negotiations.

April 27 and 30, 1981 - Two suspected arson fires cause $625,000 in damages to the administrative offices at Driftwood Middle School. Eighteen months later, a disgruntled 15-year-old and former student is charged with the crimes.

July 3, 1981 - After a sewer line in the Lakes Section breaks and spews raw sewage out of over 100 manholes, former professional diver Jim Ward is called upon to scuba dive into the sewers. Acknowledging that "the waste water made it unpleasant," Ward eventually located and repaired a fourteen inch hole. The next day, Ward admitted that "I've had five showers since midnight and I also gargled with rum four or five times."

July 31, 1981 – An early morning fire destroys Johnson Street Bowling.

May 28, 1982 - Fire Chief Edward Race announces his June retirement after twenty-six years of service in the Department. Rescue Division Chief Jim Ward is selected as his replacement.

July 1, 1982 - Union President Douglas Macready leads twenty other fire fighters in pouring 180,000 nickels and dimes into a barrel in front of the Hollywood City Commission. The coins comprised the first $5,000 of a state-levied $12,500 fine. Commissioner John Williams described the incident as "another page to your irresponsible history of the past."

December 23, 1982 - Following an apartment fire that kills a two-year old, the Department announces its first-ever citation for violations of the city's 1979 mandatory smoke detector ordinance. Based in part on a previous notice of violations, the property owner is found guilty and fined $500.

February 8, 1982 - The Department mourns the loss of eight year veteran Thomas Alan Park following his death from injuries sustained in an off duty automobile accident on Sheridan Street.

March 12, 1983 – Fire fighter/paramedic John Kellerman receives accolades after he parachutes 1,500 feet into stormy seas to administer aid to a boater lost at sea. Kellerman, a technical sergeant in the Air Force Reserves, responds as part of a military rescue team.

July 4, 1983 - Rescue personnel scramble after a faulty rocket from the City's annual fire works display misfires and injures four children in the crowd.

Fall 1983 - The Department purchases a customized apparatus, acquires specialized equipment and supplies, and provides specialized training to over thirty members in order to implement the Hazardous Materials Response Team.

October 27, 1983 - The second major fire occurs at the Diplomat Hotel.

February 1984 - Basic Life Support (BLS) engine company responses are instituted.

April 10, 1984 - In cooperation with the Department of Environmental Regulation, the Department participates in the first "Amnesty Days". The highly successful program permits citizens to safely dispose of hazardous materials without fear of legal reprisals.

June 16, 1984 - Police charge a Diplomat Hotel porter with arson after he confesses to starting two recent fires. In addition, he is considered a suspect in the major fire of October 1983.

September 18, 1984 - On the same day that the Diplomat Hotel reopens, a vacant gymnasium at the Hollywood Beach Hotel is engulfed by an arson fire. $1 million in damages helps spur an investigation by the National Bomb & Arson Response Team.

October 1984 - Relying on a combination of skill, and courage, fire fighters rescue Lieutenant Neil Fidler during a major fire in the pressroom of the Sun-Tattler newspaper. Lieutenant Fidler had become trapped, ran out of air and was on the verge of being overcome by smoke, when alert listeners heard his faint call for help over the radio.

November 1984 - The City Commission presents Awards of Valor to the firefighting crew that rescued Lt. Neil Fidler at the Sun-Tattler fire: Lt. Ed Moran, Driver Engineer Gary Peebles, and Firefighters Mark Claxon, Frank Wade, and Ed Cooper.

January 20, 1985 – Firefighter Guy Lanciault makes unsuccessful efforts to rescue the American Flag when the meeting hall of American Legion Post 92 is gutted by early morning fire. Five decades worth of war memorabilia and souvenirs are damaged and charred.

February 4, 1985 - The Department hires its first female Firefighter, Cindy Mansker.

April 1985 - Concern by the residents and merchants of West Hollywood increases when the seventh arson fire in the area occurs in just over a year; the perpetrator becomes know as "The Taft Street Bomber".

May 8, 1985 - Union President Douglas B. Macready dies following a long bout with leukemia. Apparatus and personnel from all over the state join in a traditional fire department funeral to honor the thirteen year veteran and longtime union official.

May 23, 1985 - Over one hundred police and fire personnel evacuate thousands of people when city workers discover a bulging tank of liquid chlorine at a sewage lift station.

September 1985 - The City Commission approves a budget mandating the first departmental lay-offs in almost sixty years. After only five months of employment, six firefighters lose their jobs.

September 1985 - The Hollywood Firefighters Softball Team beats out ninety other teams to win the Muscular Dystrophy Association's National Firefighters' Softball Tournament in College Park, Maryland. Steve Newmark and John Keelan are named tournament All-Stars.

Spring 1986 - While one crew battles the blaze, a second crew faces the smoke and flame from a burning Temple Beth Shalom in order to save the temple's sacred Torahs. With their success, Rabbi Morton Malavsky says "The first service we'll have is a prayerful service thanking God for being good to us."

September 1986 - The Hollywood Firefighters Softball Team prevails over eighty-four other teams to successfully defend its championship at the Muscular Dystrophy Association's National Firefighters' Softball Tournament in College Park, Maryland. It becomes the first team in tournament history to go undefeated and Steve Luongo is named the tournament's Most Valuable Player.

November 7, 1986 - Mack Industries suffers the worst fire in several years and loses its 30,000 square foot warehouse to

the million dollar blaze. Seven lengths of fire hose fail due to mildew and dry rot, prompting the emergency purchase of new hose and the installation of ventilator fans in the department's hose tower.

February 13, 1987 - The department suffers its first line of duty death in thirty-five years when twenty-three year veteran Loran "Corky" Cochran succumbs to a heart attack while inspecting the new Presidential Towers project. "Corky" is remembered for his humor and playful mischief. The Fire Fighter of the Year Award would not only be awarded to him after his death but would be renamed the Loran "Corky" Cochran Fire Fighter of the Year Award.

April 1, 1987 - Hoyt Holden helps initiate a fund-raising drive to assist in restoring "Alfie", a 1925 American LaFrance pumper apparatus which was the City's first piece of fire equipment.

June 17, 1987 - The First Baptist Church in West Hollywood suffers serious damage after maintenance men accidentally ignite a fire in the building. They had been attempting to burn a wasp's nest.

September 2, 1988 - Recently retired driver engineer/paramedic William Matthews receives the American Heart Association Award of Commendation after performing life-saving CPR on a seventy-eight year old heart attack victim he spotted while driving down Taft Street.

October 19, 1988 - Following a five month, $9,000 restoration, a 1925 American La France fire engine is presented to the Hollywood Historical Society. The engine was the Department's very first piece of firefighting apparatus.

January 13, 1989 - The fifty-three year old Royal Palm Hotel burns from a suspected arson fire, leaving one tenant dead and twenty-nine others homeless. The once luxurious hotel had become a haven for transients and drug dealers.

May 23, 1989 - The Great Southern Hotel is cited with 188 code violations as part of an enforcement sweep of the downtown area. It begins a legal battle that eventually closes the 65-year-old hotel.

May 31, 1989 - The first fatal accident involving departmental apparatus occurs when a driver makes an illegal turn in front of a rescue unit. The driver is killed and five people, including all three rescue crew members sustain injuries.

June 27, 1989 - Firefighters make a magnificent "stop" after fire enters the common roof of a 110-unit apartment complex at 4300 Sheridan Street. The damage is confined to only one wing and no more than $50,000 in losses.

August 19, 1989 - A two-story apartment building at 101 Hollywood Boulevard is destroyed by a suspected arson fire. Built in the early 1920's and scheduled for renovation, the building joined Joseph Young's home as one of the first two structures ever erected along the Boulevard.

1995 – The Citizen's Emergency Response Team (C.E.R.T) was developed to provide the citizens of Hollywood with the necessary emergency response training to provide assistance to the Fire Department when disasters strike.

1995 – The Hollywood Fire Rescue Department merges with the Beach Safety Division of the Parks, Recreation and Cultural Arts Department to become the Hollywood Fire Rescue and Beach Safety Department.

1995 – The Hollywood Fire Explorer Program was established to provide young adults who may have an interest in the Fire Service; with the opportunity to develop the knowledge, skill and abilities needed to be successful should they choose to pursue a career in the field.

January 2002 – Hollywood Fire Rescue opens "new" Fire Station 74 on Stirling Road which houses Fire Administration, Station 74, Communications, the City's Emergency Operation Center and Dania Beach Fire Rescue's Station 93. "Old Station 74 now becomes a training facility.

September 6, 2003 – At a first ever joint celebration Hollywood Fire-Rescue and Dania Beach Fire Rescue honor the new retirees of both departments. The event is held at the Westin Diplomat Resort & Spa on Hollywood Beach and also recognizes active employees' years of service, promotions and new employees hired by each department.

July 7, 2005 – Susan Thomas is the first woman in the Department's history to be promoted to Driver/Engineer.

September 22, 2005 – The Department sponsor's its first Promotional Ceremony. Twenty-six individuals were recognized for their achievements.

October 2005 – Newly constructed Fire Station 105 located on Fletcher Street and Federal Highway opens. The station houses a rescue, an engine and an aerial ladder.

January 2006 – Marine Safety Office Patrick Hendrick receives the first Employee of the Year award from the Department.

November 9, 2006 - Demolition of Station 31 begins to the 42 year old structure in preparation for a brand new facility.

An effective and well-defined administrative structure is key to the success of the Hollywood Fire/Rescue and Beach Safety Department. The coordination provided through the Administration Division, supports the Department's emergency operations. The Department's top administrative position is the Fire Chief. As the department head, and the primary representative of the department whether he is interacting with outside government agencies or citizens within our own local community.

The Deputy Chief is a hands-on administrative position, which provides the Fire Chief with executive summaries of daily operations. The Deputy Chief oversees the four major divisions of the fire department and assumes the role of acting fire chief when required.

There are four major divisions of organizational responsibility (each division is managed by a Division Chief) There are; Administration, Operations, Support Services, and the Division of Fire Prevention and Life Safety. The Division of Fire Prevention and Life Safety perform inspections plan review, investigations, public education, and respond to public information requests. The Operations Division' primary responsibility is the timely mitigation of emergency incidents such as fire, EMS & Haz-Mat. Support Service manages emergency medical services, training, and Beach Safety. The Administration Division manages information services/technical support, budget preparation, finance & procurement, and logistics.

By bringing these diverse service functions together in a smooth and productive manner, Fire Administration remain the nexus of all fire department operations.

Virgil Fernandez
Fire Chief

SERVING 6/1/2005 SINCE

Joseph Rohan
Deputy Chief

SERVING 4/4/1977 SINCE

The Command Staff is comprised of: (Front L to R) Division Chief Joseph Gambino, Division Chief Lamar Davis, Deputy Fire Chief Joseph Rohan, Fire Chief Virgil Fernandez, Division Chief Charles Barbera, Division & Division Chief Robert Aspinall. (Back L to R) Battalion Chief Martin Cooper, Battalion Chief Jeffrey Davidson, Battalion Chief David Danko, Battalion Chief Morris James, Battalion Chief Mark Steele, & Battalion Chief Gary Smith.

Lisa Blouin
Technical Business Analyst
SERVING 2/13/1995 SINCE

Beverly Busenbarrick
Administrative Assistant II
SERVING 4/19/1982 SINCE

Sandra Saffran
Administrative Assistant II
SERVING 2/20/2007 SINCE

Tanya Bouloy
Administrative Secretary
SERVING 5/24/1999 SINCE

Christine Woodward
Administrative Secretary
SERVING 4/2/1986 SINCE

Judi Anderson
Secretary
SERVING 12/22/80 SINCE

Rodger Holoubek
Chaplin
SERVING 3/1/2005 SINCE

Garland Robertson
Chaplin
SERVING 3/1/2005 SINCE

Chief Fernandez speaks to line personnel at one of many "Town Hall" meetings held by the Chief throughout the year

Charged with staffing the reception desk, Judi Anderson takes things one call at a time

Lisa Blouin and Chief Lamar Davis review a districting map

Chief Fernandez and Chief Rohan discuss daily operations

Father Rodger Holoubek gives the invocation at a Promotional Ceremony

ADMINISTRATIVE DIVISION

The Administration Division manages information services/technical support, budget preparation, financial management & procurement, construction projects, communications, Grants, research and development, equipment and facility maintenance and logistics. The coordination provided through the Administration Division, supports the Department's emergency operations.

The success of any organization requires a team of individuals working together to achieve a positive result. The Hollywood Fire Rescue and Beach Safety Department is no exception. A key component of the Administration Division is the Logistics section which is responsible for providing the resources needed to operate this Class One Department. Logistics provides equipment and supplies necessary to perform various department functions while considering quality, functionality, safety and cost. Employees who have served in the Logistics section know, without any reservation, that this is one of the most task oriented sections within the workings of any Fire Department. Their responsibilities, though wide and varied, are specific and affect the daily operations of the department.

Logistics maintains a comfortable living environment for almost 300 sworn and non-sworn personnel at six fire stations, fire administration and beach safety, and provides all of the tools, equipment and supplies required to perform their duties. Logistics is also responsible for maintaining, repairing and inspecting the department's more than 110 Fire Rescue, Beach Safety and Support vehicles.

In November of 2004, the citizens of the City of Hollywood approved a $25 million General Obligation Bond for the Fire Rescue and Beach Safety Department. Funding was earmarked for the replacement of fire apparatus and the rebuilding of five Fire Rescue facilities. In April 2006, the Department accepted delivery of a new 100 foot aerial platform truck and a fire pumper from Pierce Manufacturing Inc. Both vehicles are state of the art in technology which allows Fire Rescue personnel to operate with greater efficiency and safety.

Charles Barbera
Division Chief
SERVING 10/4/1976 SINCE

Gary Smith
Battalion Chief
SERVING 6/15/1981 SINCE

Lawrence Allwine
Lieutenant
SERVING 5/24/1982 SINCE

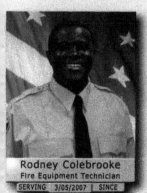

Rodney Colebrooke
Fire Equipment Technician
SERVING 3/05/2007 SINCE

Max Diah
Hydrant Technician
SERVING 12/1/2003 SINCE

Janet Gurdyal
Administrative Secretary
SERVING 1/3/1989 SINCE

Judi Ramos
Storekeeper
SERVING 1/9/2006 SINCE

Peter Robinson
Firefighter
SERVING 10/4/1976 SINCE

Rodney Colebrooke, Herb Helfen, Judi Ramos, & Pete Robinson take a few minutes to grab lunch.

Pete Robinson maintains the oxygen tanks at Station 74.

City Manager Cameron Benson presents Lt. Larry Allwine with the City's Diamond Service Award

Lt. Larry Allwine welcomes Father Rodger Holoubek and Pastor Garland Robertson as the Department's Chaplins

MAINTENANCE

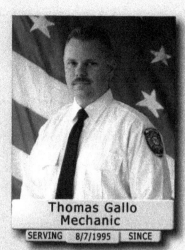

Thomas Gallo
Mechanic
SERVING 8/7/1995 SINCE

Michael Cross
Mechanic
SERVING 8/28/2006 SINCE

Ganga Parma
Mechanic
SERVING 7/15/1996 SINCE

Mechanic Ganga Parma checks Rescue 74

Chief Mechanic Tom Gallo gets ready to conduct a flow test on an engine

Mechanic Mike Cross changes a belt on Rescue 45

Ganga, Tom, and Mike help to keep both Dania & Hollywood units running

In the late 1950's, the Hollywood Fire Department began providing emergency medical service in addition to fire protection. They attended basic first aid training off duty and procured a used Hearse from a local funeral parlor for use as the Department's first emergency medical response vehicle.

As the demand for emergency services increased, the Department hired additional personnel who received both fire fighting and Basic Life Support (BLS) training. Quality Emergency Medical Response was attained in the mid-1970s and the name was changed to the Hollywood Fire/Rescue Department.

Hollywood Fire/Rescue became involved with Advanced Life Support (ALS) emergency medicine in its infancy. In 1964, when Dr. Eugene Nagel began speaking about using firefighters in the field as the eyes and the hands of emergency room physicians, Hollywood Fire/Rescue was eager to participate.

In 1984, a Basic Life Support (BLS) program was instituted on all fire engines which were staffed by at least one EMT or paramedic. Currently, the Department's six fire engines are BLS equipped and staffed with both paramedics and EMT's. These units respond to medical emergencies when the regularly assigned ALS Rescue is out of the district or when extra personnel are needed on scene. This system has proved to be a more timely and efficient means of delivering emergency medical service to the public. The EMS service is also an integral part in the Broward County Trauma Care Network. This network of hospitals and emergency service agencies provides victims of traumatic accidents with the most rapidly available treatment and transport to specialized trauma centers throughout Broward County.

The Hollywood Fire/Rescue and Beach Safety Department currently employs 275 personnel 223 of which are certified firefighters who are either EMTs or paramedics. Since 1986 when labor and management agreed that all new personnel must become a paramedic within the first four years of their employment, it has been the Department's goal to have all line personnel certified as paramedics. This reflects the Department's commitment to educate all department personnel in the delivery of Advanced Life Support from the Fire Chief down to the newest recruit.

Hollywood personnel have been actively involved in the legislative and regulatory process of statewide EMS protocols and procedures and have consistently shown a commitment to patient care over any other consideration. A local ordinance was instituted in 1993 that requires an ALS Rescue to respond to any emergency medical call to "911" in the City of Hollywood. This demonstrates the city Commission's and fire department's willingness to provide the most advanced system of pre-hospital care available. In 1994 the State of Florida Department of Health established the "EMS Provider of the Year and the Hollywood Fire Rescue Department was its first recipient. In 2005 the Hollywood Fire/Rescue and Beach Safety Department responded to 20,032 calls for emergency medical service.

Lamar Davis
Division Chief
SERVING 5/22/1978 SINCE

Daniel Blundy
Training Officer
SERVING 10/4/1976 SINCE

Bonnie Hogue
Administrative Secretary
SERVING 11/23/1992 SINCE

Medical Director Dr. Richard Dellerson, oversees the medical protocols followed by Support Services

Jeane Romano, Dr. Dellerson's assistant keeps him up to date with all the paperwork.

Support Services is responsible for making sure that all life support apparatus have the necessary medical equipment needed for the treatment of patients.

Bonnie Hogue (ret.), Dan Blundy, Lamar Davis meet to discuss a records management issue.

TRAINING

Prior to 1968, the Hollywood Fire Rescue and Beach Safety Department lacked a formal recruit training program. New hires were simply assigned a combat position under the direct supervision of a company officer who was responsible for recruit on-the-job training. Training mainly focused on climbing aerial ladders and operating high-pressure hose lines. The "drill ground" simply referred to utilizing cleared parking lots and dead-end streets.

In October of 1976, the Hollywood Fire College opened a new recruit training facility in the City of Hollywood's Wastewater Treatment Plant at 14th Avenue and Taft Street. Although the facility grounds were not necessarily conducive to the training needs of the department, diverse rudimentary simulations of fire ground operations such as structure fires, liquefied petroleum gas fires, and search and rescue operations were made possible. The facility also supported enough space to facilitate hose, driver/engineer and aerial training.

Although Dale Rose was the Department's first training officer, the fire college concept evolved under the direction of Division Chief George Warren. The Hollywood Fire College eventually became known as the Training Section under the umbrella of the Support Services Division, where some of the most diverse training programs are delivered. Its success today is attributed to the endeavors and commitment of past and present Training personnel.

In October 1982, the Training Section developed and submitted for state approval an Emergency Vehicle Operator's Course (EVOC) which was adopted in 1983 by the state as a model for future Health and Rehabilitative Services (HRS) regulations. In addition, the department received HRS approval for a forty-nine hour in-service, Continuing Education Unit (CEU) paramedic recertification program developed by the Training Section. This concept eventually expanded and included an Emergency Medical Technicians (EMTs) program, both of which continue today.

In the late 1980's, Training expanded its area of responsibility by becoming a Community Training Center for Cardio Pulmonary Resuscitation (CPR), and continues to provide instruction to both the private sector and other city departments.

The Training Section manages, develops and implements comprehensive training programs necessary to help maintain the department's Insurance Service Organization (ISO) Class 1 rating.

Mark Steele
Battalion Chief
SERVING   9/5/1983   SINCE

Joel Medina
Training Officer
SERVING   11/7/1994   SINCE

Jorge Castano
Training Instructor
SERVING   3/1/1993   SINCE

While in training, new recruits learn how to lay hose

Training Instructor Jorge Castano gets "The Maze Room" ready

Recruit Dawn Clarke awaits her turn at climbing up the ladder

Training Officer Joel Medina goes over the symptoms of Cardiomyopathy during CEUs

Rescue Diver Chris Sullivan waits for direction during dive training

29

Battalion Chief Mark Steele teaches a NIMS class to City employees

Backup Diver Geza Hegedus keeps a watchful eye on the Rescue & Safety Divers

A recruit prepares to hook up a 5" hose to the hydrant

David Guernsey takes a break during dive rescue training

Battalion Chief Mark Steele reviews a new DVD training series with Training Officer Joel Medina and Training Instructor Jorge Castano

RECRUIT CLASSES

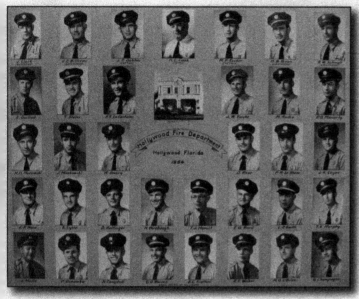

1954

February 1975

October 1972

October 1976

January 1977

April 1977

May 1978

April 1979

June 1981

January 1982

May 1982

January 1989

November 1994

May 1999

November 2001

April 2002

November 2002

November 2003

August 2004

January 2005

July 2005

October 2005

November 2005

September 2006

July 2007

February 2008

A recruit gets a feel for "Black Out" conditions by navigating "The Maze Room"

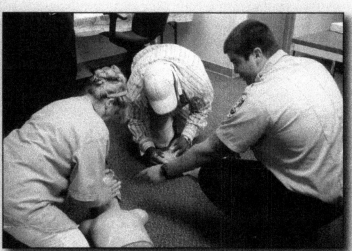

Recruit Mike Gulla helps to teach a CPR class

BEACH SAFETY

In an effort to enhance the delivery of emergency service to the citizens of the City of Hollywood and its visitors, Beach Safety and the Department of Fire Rescue merged in 1995. Under the auspices of the Fire Chief, Beach Safety is a critical component of the full compliment of services provided by the fire department. It is under the direct supervision of the Division Chief of Support Services who is responsible for managing and overseeing the daily operations.

To ensure public safety along the four and one-half miles of beachfront property, twenty lifeguard towers are strategically placed along the City's coastal waters to help facilitate an immediate response to emergencies, or to summon supplementary Fire Rescue resources, if necessary. Beach Safety personnel have adopted a proactive approach to protecting bathers by enforcing regulations and policies, and are cognizant of the ever-changing water conditions. As a result, Hollywood Beach Safety has been named the top Beach Safety Division in the State of Florida twice by the Florida Beach Patrol Chief's Association, and boasts one of the top safety records on the state and national level.

Beach Safety personnel incessantly train to effectively provide the safest experience for beachgoers. Annual refresher training is provided for Emergency Medical Technician (EMT) recertification, First Responder and Cardio Pulmonary Resuscitation (CPR). The Division was one of the first in the country to meet the standards for the Advanced Agency Rating awarded by the United States Lifesaving Association. USLA standards include medical certifications, training standard equipment and physical guidelines. In addition, Beach Safet personnel are required to maintain top physical conditionin to meet the demands necessary for life-saving measures. Twic a year, members participate in mandatory physical abilit testing consisting of a one-half mile sand run and a one-hal mile ocean swim. As a result of this physical conditioning Hollywood lifeguards representing the City of Hollywood i the annual Corporate Run competition have historically take first place among the thousands of competitors.

Beach Safety employs a broad spectrum of specialize equipment and apparatus to facilitate their mission an provide the best possible service to the public. All-terrai vehicles, jet skis, rescue boards, surf skis, emergency medic equipment and Automated External Defibrillators (A.E.D.s are immediately available in the event of an emergency.

Community involvement, education, physical an academic training, and the development and implementatio of Standard Operating Procedures (SOPs), are only a few c the key elements responsible for the success of Beach Safety Through accomplished programs such as the Junior Lifeguar program, mentoring young adults from local high schools speaking to community groups and leaders, and activ participation in lifeguard programs and competitions, th City of Hollywood Beach Safety Division is recognized as on of the top Beach Safety programs in the state.

James Shoemaker
MS Chief
SERVING 3/26/1978 SINCE

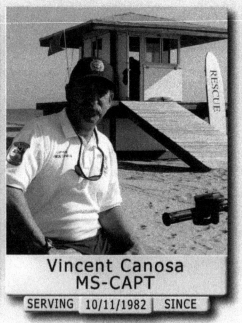

Vincent Canosa
MS-CAPT
SERVING 10/11/1982 SINCE

Patrick Hendrick
MS-LT
SERVING 9/28/1981 SINCE

Cathy Laucella
MS LT
SERVING 7/11/1994 SINCE

Michael McManus
MS-LT
SERVING 2/24/1986 SINCE

Mark Mullen
LT-MSO
SERVING 10/20/1986 SINCE

Joseph Taylor
MS-LT
SERVING 6/1/1987 SINCE

Alan Beech
MSO
SERVING 6/30/1997 SINCE

Jose Bolivar
MSO
SERVING 9/11/2006 SINCE

Jill Cambra
Lifeguard
SERVING 9/25/1997 SINCE

David Carpenter
Lifeguard
SERVING 6/9/1984 SINCE

Kevin Channer
Lifeguard
SERVING 10/7/1994 SINCE

Andrea Cross
MSO
SERVING 7/9/2007 SINCE

Istvan Csendes
Lifeguard
SERVING 12/9/2004 SINCE

Louis Desimone
MSO
SERVING 1/30/1995 SINCE

Tom Dollinger
Lifeguard
SERVING 11/1/1995 SINCE

Jeff Epstein
MSS
SERVING 1/3/1995 SINCE

Bryan Ferguson
MSO
SERVING 8/24/1998 SINCE

Richard Fiorillo
MSO
SERVING 7/3/1995 SINCE

Jenny Garcia
Lifeguard
SERVING 11/28/2005 SINCE

Juan Garcia
Lifeguard
SERVING 8/6/1998 SINCE

Ernesto Gomez
Lifeguard
SERVING 7/13/2000 SINCE

Leonardo Gonzalez
Lifeguard
SERVING 11/5/2001 SINCE

Rodolfo Gonzalez
Lifeguard
SERVING 11/28/2005 SINCE

Mario Jelev
Lifeguard
SERVING 6/30/2000 SINCE

Kaley Lucas
Lifeguard
SERVING 10/27/2003 SINCE

Francis Lynch
MSO
SERVING 7/3/1995 SINCE

Kevin MacKinlay
Lifeguard
SERVING 7/31/2003 SINCE

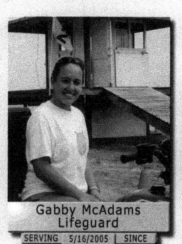

Fernando Marrero
Lifeguard
SERVING 9/29/2003 SINCE

Gabby McAdams
Lifeguard
SERVING 5/16/2005 SINCE

Joyce O'Brien
Lifeguard
SERVING 8/22/2005 SINCE

Diego O'Campo
Lifeguard
SERVING 3/13/2006 SINCE

Robert Ormston
Lifeguard
SERVING 11/7/2003 SINCE

Sergio Palacio
Lifeguard
SERVING 1/15/1996 SINCE

Edward Perrin
MSO
SERVING 11/1/1999 SINCE

Raymond Pichardo
Lifeguard
SERVING 7/18/2005 SINCE

Sal Polistina
MSO
SERVING 3/11/1991 SINCE

Petko Prachtakov
Lifeguard
SERVING 11/5/2001 SINCE

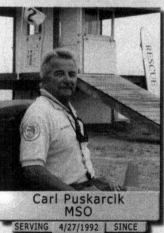

Carl Puskarcik
MSO
SERVING 4/27/1992 SINCE

Eddie Robledo
MSO
SERVING 11/13/1995 SINCE

Pete Thompson
Lifeguard
SERVING 12/27/2004 SINCE

James Turner
MSO
SERVING 7/18/1988 SINCE

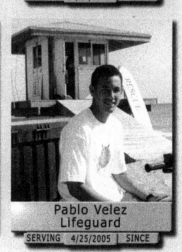

Pablo Velez
Lifeguard
SERVING 4/25/2005 SINCE

Mark Vezi
Lifeguard
SERVING 7/21/2003 SINCE

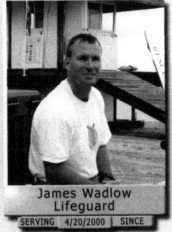

James Wadlow
Lifeguard
SERVING 4/20/2000 SINCE

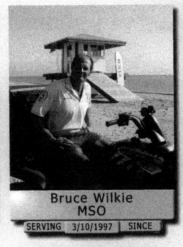

Bruce Wilkie
MSO
SERVING 3/10/1997 SINCE

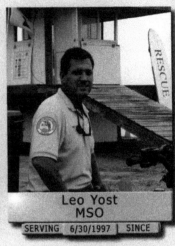

Leo Yost
MSO
SERVING 6/30/1997 SINCE

The AED is applied and CPR begins

Lifeguard Fernando Marrero, Lifeguard Nick Macko, Chief Virgil Fernandez and Marine Safety Chief Jim Shoemaker congratulate Pat Hendrick on receiving the Employee of the Year Award.

Keeping watch on Hollywood beach

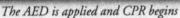

Lifeguard Jose Bolivar gets ready to demonstrate pulling a drowning victim from the water to elementary school children

Lt. Alan Beech patrols the beach

Marine Safety Chief Jim Shoemaker and Nick "Mako" Macko talk to Open House attendees about Beach Safety operations

Beach Safety members display their awards after dominating the 2006 Corporate Run

Bruce Wilkie helps to supervise the Junior Lifeguard program

Beach Safety personnel attend a training class

Lifeguards Jim Wadlow and Kaley Lucas keep a close eye on swimmers during a rip current warning

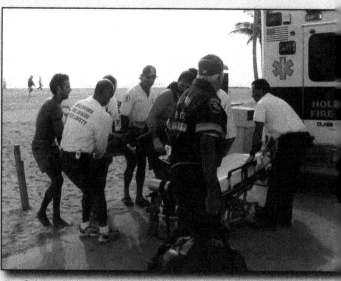

The Beach Safety team log roll a drowning victim onto the backboard

Firefighters Gary Lehmann, Ray Wagner and Lieutenant Alex P[...] prepare to take over patient care

Lifeguard Jim Wadlow and Lieutenant Pat Hendrick receive their awards for Lifeguard of the Year and Employee of the Year respectively.

Lieutenant Joe Taylor goes over the day's assignments at morning line up

BUREAU OF FIRE PREVENTION & LIFE SAFETY

The Bureau of Fire Prevention and Life Safety, was established in the 1950's by the Hollywood Fire Department in accordance with the evolution of standardized codes in Broward County. Shortly thereafter, an extensive filing system encompassing all commercial and multi-residential structures was initiated. Bureau personnel were assigned an office at City Hall working closely with the Building Department and Code Enforcement divisions; a relationship which is still enjoyed today. In addition, inspectors were trained to work in conjunction with Hollywood Police Detectives investigating incendiary fires.

In 1957, the South Florida Building Code was adopted by the Broward County Commission. At that time, Hollywood had in place its own building code which included chapters on fire construction standards, fire protection equipment and life safety features for structures.

During the 1960's a process began whereby each city adopted the South Florida Building Code. In 1972, a special act established minimum requirements for the certification of fire inspectors. These requirements enabled the Fire Marshal's Office to maintain and enforce the highest level of life safety standards available with professionally qualified inspectors.

Presently, the Division consists of two secretaries, one plans examiner, nine inspectors, a Deputy Fire Marshal and a Fire Marshal. They are responsible for managing over 9,500 active building files which are broken down into districts, special buildings or occupancy classifications, and all licensed hazardous material facilities. Each structure, with the exception of single family homes and duplexes, is inspected annually and its inspection report is filed for future comparison.

With the goal of reducing the loss of life and property from the destruction of fire being a priority, Bureau staff performs various activities designed to provide steady measurable progress. These activities are classified as follows: preconstruction plans review, Fire Investigations, Fire Inspections, and Public Education.

The process of building Life Safety into our community starts in the pre-planning stages of construction. Construction plans are reviewed by the Department's Broward County certified fire plans examiners. A positive working relationship with architects, engineers, contractors, and building owners goes hand in hand with the recent redevelopment in Hollywood. Once buildings are completed, inspectors assure compliance with maintenance of Life Safety systems and practices and all adopted codes through continuous on-site inspections and follow-up inspections.

Outreach programs offering people the opportunity to receive Life Safety information have grown over the years. Fire Prevention Week is but one example of a Public Educational outreach program activity aimed at reducing loss of life and reducing property loss through education. Safety Town, established at TY Park in Hollywood by the Joe DiMaggio Children's Hospital at Memorial Regional Hospital, is another example of the many public education initiatives conducted by the Fire Marshal's Office.

Robert Aspinall
Division Chief
SERVING 6/8/1981 SINCE

Eric Busenbarrick
FPO III
SERVING 10/07/1991 SINCE

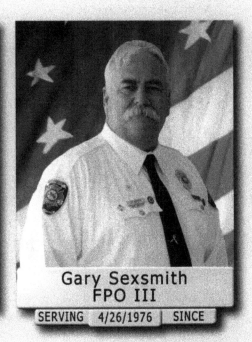

Gary Sexsmith
FPO III
SERVING 4/26/1976 SINCE

Jay Havens
FPO II
SERVING 1/3/1989 SINCE

Robert Hazen
FPO II
SERVING 7/6/1981 SINCE

Mack Moore
FPO II
SERVING 9/18/1995 SINCE

Matthew Phillips
FPO II
SERVING 8/11/1976 SINCE

Janet Washburn
FPO II
SERVING 9/21/1998 SINCE

Mark Fritz
FPO I
SERVING 9/18/1995 SINCE

Roy White
FPO I
SERVING 9/18/1995 SINCE

Kim Graves
Secretary
SERVING 12/26/2000 SINCE

Donna D'Angelo
Secretary
SERVING 2/15/1999 SINCE

Matt Phillips turns in his paperwork to Kim Graves

Chief Robert Aspinall and Secretaries Donna D'Angelo and Kim Graves go over the day's report

Roy White searches for evidence after a suspected arson fire

Mack Moore checks the expiration date on a fire extinguisher

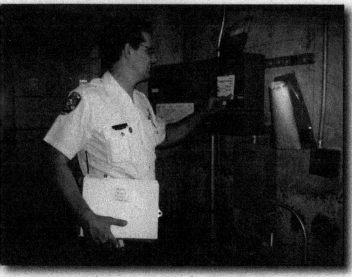

Rob Hazen inspects a fire alarm panel

Mark Fritz stops by the office to fill out his daily reports

Gary Sexsmith takes a look at plans that have just been submitted for review

The inspectors get ready to start their day

Jay Havens conducts class at Safety Town

Janet Washburn and Eric Busenbarrick assist Code Enforcement Inspectors from Plan Review

The Hollywood Fire Rescue Explorer program was established in 1995 with the efforts of Firefighters George Burns and Jose Morales. With a mission statement of "empowering and developing our youth so they may diligently lead the Fire Service on to the next alarm", the program affords individuals who may have an interest in the Fire Service as a career, the opportunity to develop the knowledge, skills, and abilities required for such an endeavor. It is a value-driven effort which embraces the values of service and responsibility, and develops the leadership potential within our youth. This invaluable program, along with many of our firefighters who have unselfishly volunteered their time throughout the years to support our Explorers, has been responsible for mentoring numerous firefighters who are currently serving with our department and the communities throughout Florida.

The following is a list of former Explorers currently employed as fire fighters with the City of Hollywood Fire Rescue and Beach Safety Department:

Dave Guernsey
Kevin Dodds
Josh Wells
Chris Coxe
Rita Pereira
Mitchell Li

The above statement is dedicated to Rick Ragusa and Tim Burke, Explorers who tragically lost their lives before fulfilling their dreams of serving as firefighters, but who nonetheless served our community and country admirably.

The "Employee of the Year" award is presented to non-sworn personnel for rendering excellent service to the public or their co-workers, while serving as a positive role model throughout the prior year. Annual nominations a submitted to the Diamond Bright Committee for review an a recommendation is sent to the Fire Chief for final approva

Patrick Hendrick – 2005

Tom Gallo - 2006

Juan Restrepo - 2007

The "Firefighter of the Year" award is presented to sworn personnel for rendering excellent service to the public or their co-workers, while serving as a positive role model throughout the prior year. Annual nominations are now submitted to the Diamond Bright Committee for review by all department personnel and a recommendation is sent to the Fire Chief for final approval.

Albert Gilbert
1976

Thomas Mikell
1977

Donald Perdue
1978

Edward Moran
1979, 1981

William Barr
1979

Ronald Shulby
1980

Wayne Mailliard
1982

Daniel Fitzgerald
1983

John Kellerman
1984

Loran Cochran
1985

Thomas Karl
1986

Robert Allen
1987

Neil Fidler
1988

John McMillan
1989

Gary Peebles
1990

Stephen Newmark
1991

Robert Madge
1992

Gary Smith
1993

Matthew Phillips
1994

Donald Barfield
1995

John Shelton
1996

Brian White
1997

Joseph Gambino
1998

Thomas Dinges
1999

Jose Morales
2000

Douglas Brown
2001

Wayne Bruce
2002

Dennis O'Toole
2003

Peter Robinson
2004

Anthony Liddell
2005

Lawrence Latore
2006

Diana DeAbreu
2007

OPERATIONS

The Operations Division of the Hollywood Fire Rescue and Beach Safety Department is directed by the Division Chief of Operations who is responsible for managing and overseeing the diverse disciplines of the Operations component of the Department. Fire suppression, emergency medical incidents, hazardous materials response and technical rescue are only a few of the broad spectrum of services provided by the Operations Division.

The uniformed men and women of the Operations Division respond from six stations and provide the necessary coverage and resources to successfully manage and control in excess of 27,000 emergency incidents annually. The Division's 200 certified firefighter paramedics are assigned to three shifts staffing six Basic Life Support (BLS) engine companies, seven Advance Life Support (ALS) rescue units and three aerial ladder companies. Daily activities and emergency responses are under direct supervision of a Battalion Chief.

All Stations operate with BLS engine companies equipped to provide on-scene pre-hospital emergency medical care and patient stabilization. Advance Life Support/Transport rescue units are equipped with the latest in medical equipment and, under the direction of a Medical Director, are able to administer medications necessary to meet the challenges of today's ever-changing advanced cardiac life support and pre-hospital patient care.

The Division maintains a hazardous materials response capability for the control and mitigation of toxic substance releases. The team is equipped with a wide range of specialized protective clothing and is complimented by sophisticated computerized detection and sampling devices to help identify unknown products. Mutual Aid and Interlocal Agreements are in place providing the mechanism for county and state wide emergency response. An association with local, state and federal agencies help facilitate critical planning, formulation and implementation of common county and state-wide policies and procedures.

Public education, facility inspections and daily fire related training all contribute to the Division's primary mission to protect and serve the public and to provide the services necessary to successfully prevent the loss of life and property.

Joseph Gambino
Operations Chief

SERVING   4/4/1977   SINCE

A 911 call is answered by a Telecommunicator I "Call Taker"

Captain David Austin and Firefighter Steve Ciorrocco check for fire extension

Firefighter Jack Saunders tends the line while the rescue diver searches the water for a drowning victim.

Engine 31 responds to a rollover at I-595 and the Turnpike

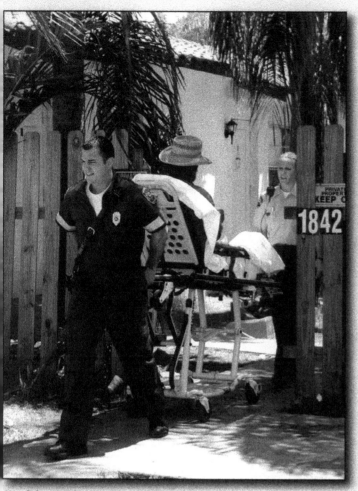

After the Call Taker has received the pertinent information this information is then routed to a Telecommunicatetor ll "Dispatcher" for station notification.

Firefighters John Manos and Marcy Treadwell assist a patient to a waiting Rescue 5.

Sue Thomas receives her Driver Engineer badge from Chief Fernandez

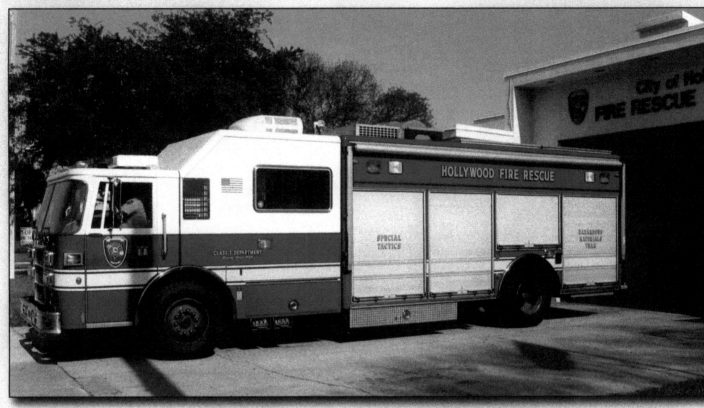

Driver Engineer Bill Jones rolls out to another Haz-Mat call.

Captain Bill Major looks on as Firefighter Chris Taylor, and Firefighter Abi Montes trauma alert an accident victim.

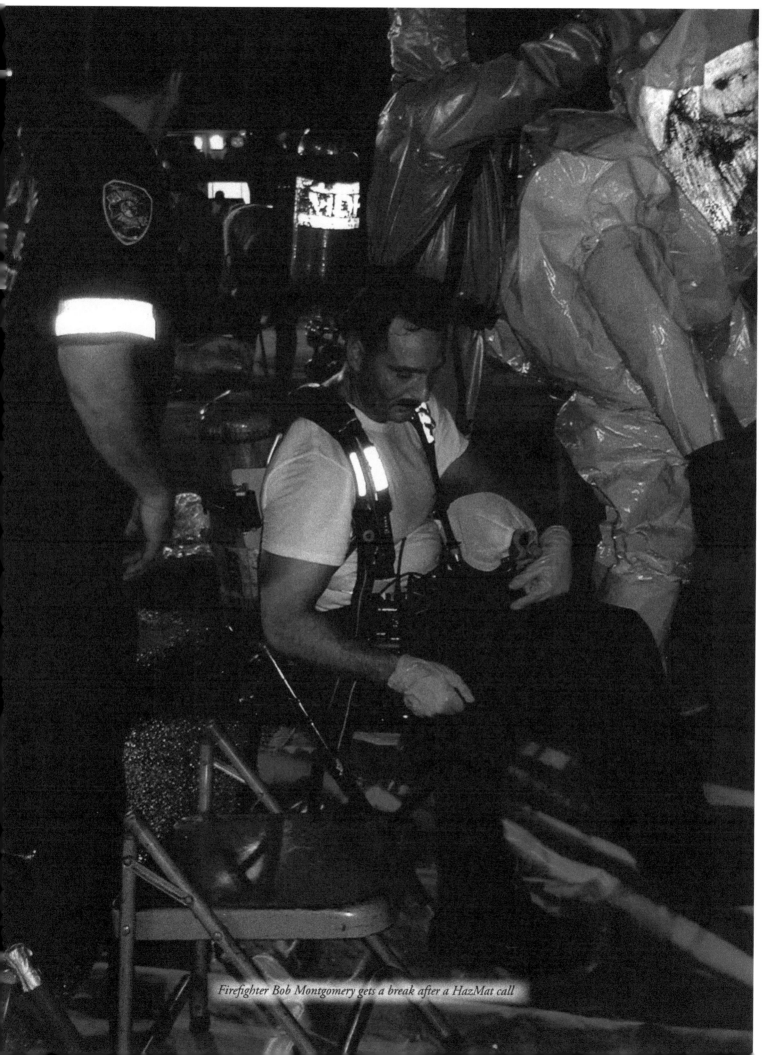

Firefighter Bob Montgomery gets a break after a HazMat call

Martin Cooper
Battalion Chief
SERVING 4/4/1977 SINCE

David Danko
Battalion Chief
SERVING 2/4/1980 SINCE

Jeffrey Davidson
Battalion Chief
SERVING 10/24/1988 SINCE

Morris James
Battalion Chief
SERVING 11/24/1980 SINCE

David Austin
Captain
SERVING 1/4/1982 SINCE

Richard Barnett
Captain
SERVING 1/3/1977 SINCE

Robert Bazy
Captain
SERVING 5/22/1978 SINCE

John Bridenburg
Captain

SERVING | 1/27/1986 | SINCE

Jay Bryan
Captain

SERVING | 4/5/1976 | SINCE

Louis Carman
Captain

SERVING | 10/4/1976 | SINCE

Mark Claxon
Captain

SERVING | 4/30/1979 | SINCE

Charles Colson
Captain

SERVING | 7/20/1987 | SINCE

Patrick Croghan
Captain

SERVING | 10/5/1987 | SINCE

Kenneth Delbert
Captain

SERVING | 11/24/1980 | SINCE

Thomas Dinges
Captain

SERVING | 4/4/1977 | SINCE

Gary Ethridge
Captain

SERVING | 2/4/1980 | SINCE

63

Daniel Fitzgerald
Captain
SERVING | 1/3/1977 | SINCE

John Johnson
Captain
SERVING | 11/24/1980 | SINCE

James Jones
Captain
SERVING | 11/24/1980 | SINCE

John Kuklinski
Captain
SERVING | 11/3/1986 | SINCE

Guy Lanciault
Captain
SERVING | 10/4/1976 | SINCE

William Major
Captain
SERVING | 1/24/1983 | SINCE

Jose Morales
Captain
SERVING | 4/13/1992 | SINCE

Robert Munson
Captain
SERVING | 4/1/1974 | SINCE

Raymond Powers
Captain
SERVING | 3/20/1978 | SINCE

Christopher Pratt
Captain
SERVING   10/2/1989   SINCE

Norman Rechtman
Captain
SERVING   4/4/1977   SINCE

Dennis Rudasill
Captain
SERVING   1/17/1983   SINCE

Joseph Stolarz
Captain
SERVING   5/12/1975   SINCE

David Swick
Captain
SERVING   5/22/1978   SINCE

Robert Arndt
Lieutenant
SERVING   1/24/1983   SINCE

Michael Briosi
Lieutenant
SERVING   5/24/1982   SINCE

Allen Burchardt
Lieutenant
SERVING   3/20/1978   SINCE

Russell Chard
Lieutenant
SERVING 4/30/1979 SINCE

Brian Cooke
Lieutenant
SERVING 1/20/1987 SINCE

Thomas Coughlin
Lieutenant
SERVING 11/24/1980 SINCE

Marc Croteau
Lieutenant
SERVING 1/3/1989 SINCE

James Cummins
Lieutenant
SERVING 1/3/1989 SINCE

James Daniels
Lieutenant
SERVING 7/19/1982 SINCE

Mark Ellis
Lieutenant
SERVING 8/10/1987 SINCE

Michael Fulks
Lieutenant
SERVING 4/4/1977 SINCE

Philip Healey
Lieutenant
SERVING 7/19/1982 SINCE

John Hicks
Lieutenant
SERVING   5/26/1980   SINCE

Rodolfo Jurado
Lieutenant
SERVING   1/8/1996   SINCE

John Kebler
Lieutenant
SERVING   6/8/1981   SINCE

Patrick Keller
Lieutenant
SERVING   1/3/1989   SINCE

John Kellerman
Lieutenant
SERVING   2/4/1980   SINCE

Christofer Korn
Lieutenant
SERVING   9/18/1995   SINCE

John Kusuk
Lieutenant
SERVING   10/4/1976   SINCE

Robert Ladwig
Lieutenant
SERVING   9/18/1995   SINCE

Sean McGillivray
Lieutenant
SERVING   9/18/1995   SINCE

Mark Miller
Lieutenant
SERVING 1/3/1994 SINCE

Patrick Moore
Lieutenant
SERVING 6/8/1992 SINCE

Richard Pingol
Lieutenant
SERVING 5/1/1978 SINCE

Alexander Poli
Lieutenant
SERVING 9/18/1995 SINCE

Kevin Politte
Lieutenant
SERVING 7/7/1980 SINCE

Kevin Reardon
Lieutenant
SERVING 11/24/1980 SINCE

John Saredy
Lieutenant
SERVING 6/8/1981 SINCE

David Selby
Lieutenant
SERVING 1/8/1996 SINCE

John Shelton
Lieutenant
SERVING 6/11/1990 SINCE

Ronald White
Lieutenant
SERVING 2/27/1989 SINCE

Keenan Bain
Driver Engineer
SERVING 8/9/1999 SINCE

Harry Bealmear
Driver Engineer
SERVING 1/4/1982 SINCE

William Biglin
Driver Engineer
SERVING 11/7/1994 SINCE

Michael Cardillo
Driver Engineer
SERVING 9/12/1988 SINCE

David Civita
Driver Engineer
SERVING 8/22/1988 SINCE

Mark Cowart
Driver Engineer
SERVING 6/30/1986 SINCE

Kenneth Cressler
Driver Engineer
SERVING 10/8/1984 SINCE

Daniel Dapolito
Driver Engineer

SERVING 9/18/1995 SINCE

Andrew Davis
Driver Engineer

SERVING 11/17/1997 SINCE

Diana DeAbreu
Driver Engineer

SERVING 9/18/1995 SINCE

Chris Delcampo
Driver Engineer

SERVING 1/12/1998 SINCE

Frank Emiliano
Driver Engineer

SERVING 5/22/1978 SINCE

Joseph Fisher
Driver Engineer

SERVING 5/24/1982 SINCE

Marcus Fresco
Driver Engineer

SERVING 9/18/1995 SINCE

Eric Guerrero
Driver Engineer

SERVING 5/1/1995 SINCE

Herbert Helfen
Driver Engineer

SERVING 11/24/1980 SINCE

Michael Holm
Driver Engineer
SERVING 10/13/1986 SINCE

Charles Johnson
Driver Engineer
SERVING 5/24/1976 SINCE

William Jones
Driver Engineer
SERVING 9/5/1983 SINCE

Hal Kelley
Driver Engineer
SERVING 4/7/1979 SINCE

David Knott
Driver Engineer
SERVING 7/12/1976 SINCE

Juan Lana
Driver Engineer
SERVING 1/3/1989 SINCE

Donald Lassiter
Driver Engineer
SERVING 11/21/1988 SINCE

Steven Martin
Driver Engineer
SERVING 8/3/1987 SINCE

Daniel Martinez
Driver Engineer
SERVING 4/5/1999 SINCE

Victor Monette
Driver Engineer
SERVING 10/16/1989 SINCE

Stephen Newmark
Driver Engineer
SERVING 4/4/1977 SINCE

Mark Payne
Driver Engineer
SERVING 1/3/1989 SINCE

Bernard Pflum
Driver Engineer
SERVING 8/22/1988 SINCE

Thomas Price
Driver Engineer
SERVING 1/3/1989 SINCE

Mark Ramsay
Driver Engineer
SERVING 11/24/1980 SINCE

Charles Redding
Driver Engineer
SERVING 12/11/1990 SINCE

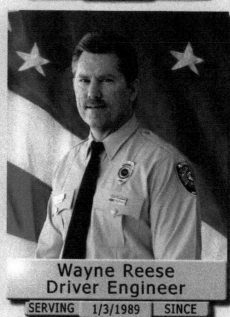

Wayne Reese
Driver Engineer
SERVING 1/3/1989 SINCE

Peter Reilly
Driver Engineer
SERVING 7/7/1980 SINCE

David Sheldon
Driver Engineer

SERVING 7/14/1986 SINCE

Paul Watson
Driver Engineer

SERVING 6/8/1981 SINCE

Brian White
Driver Engineer

SERVING 9/18/1995 SINCE

Sue Thomas
Driver Engineer

SERVING 10/26/1992 SINCE

Charles Tullio
Driver Engineer

SERVING 11/7/1994 SINCE

Richard Tursi
Driver Engineer

SERVING 7/19/1982 SINCE

Christopher Venezia
Driver Engineer

SERVING 11/24/1980 SINCE

Frank Wade
Driver Engineer

SERVING 9/5/1983 SINCE

Alan Wasserman
Driver Engineer

SERVING 6/29/1992 SINCE

Christopher Allen
Firefighter
SERVING 5/17/1999 SINCE

Joseph Amy
Firefighter
SERVING 12/4/2000 SINCE

Adam App
Firefighter
SERVING 11/21/2005 SINCE

Derek Avilez
Firefighter
SERVING 6/19/2006 SINCE

Kerry Boyett
Firefighter
SERVING 8/23/2004 SINCE

James Brito
Firefighter
SERVING 8/9/2004 SINCE

George Burns
Firefighter
SERVING 6/7/1993 SINCE

Rocio Cervini
Firefighter
SERVING 6/12/2006 SINCE

Anthony Cioppa
Firefighter
SERVING 2/26/1996 SINCE

Stephen Ciorrocco
Firefighter

SERVING | 5/22/1978 | SINCE

Dawn Clarke
Firefighter

SERVING | 12/29/2003 | SINCE

Christopher Clinton
Firefighter

SERVING | 11/10/2003 | SINCE

Christopher Coxe
Firefighter

SERVING | 11/21/2005 | SINCE

Shane Davis
Firefighter

SERVING | 2/10/2003 | SINCE

Kevin Dodds
Firefighter

SERVING | 12/13/2004 | SINCE

Sidney Doret
Firefighter

SERVING | 5/07/2007 | SINCE

David Duensing
Firefighter

SERVING | 4/5/1999 | SINCE

Phillip Edelman
Firefighter

SERVING | 11/10/2003 | SINCE

Andrew Estevez
Firefighter

SERVING | 9/3/2001 | SINCE

Brian Ettinger
Firefighter

SERVING | 11/28/2005 | SINCE

Joseph Eutsey
Firefighter

SERVING | 2/4/1980 | SINCE

Dean Eyerman
Firefighter

SERVING | 3/6/1989 | SINCE

Peter Falk
Firefighter

SERVING | 11/26/2001 | SINCE

Mark Fee
Firefighter

SERVING | 01/02/2008 | SINCE

Humberto Fernandez
Firefighter

SERVING | 11/5/2001 | SINCE

Jose Fernandez
Firefighter

SERVING | 6/16/2006 | SINCE

Rafael Fuentes
Firefighter

SERVING | 7/9/2001 | SINCE

Analdy Garcia
Firefighter
SERVING 8/21/2000 SINCE

Roberto Garcia
Firefighter
SERVING 4/13/1987 SINCE

Curtis Grier
Firefighter
SERVING 9/18/1995 SINCE

David Guernsey
Firefighter
SERVING 3/25/2002 SINCE

Michael Gulla
Firefighter
SERVING 6/12/2006 SINCE

Michael Hapsas
Firefighter
SERVING 9/23/1991 SINCE

Marlene Harden
Firefighter
SERVING 7/27/1992 SINCE

Richard Harvey
Firefighter
SERVING 2/27/1995 SINCE

Geza Hegedus
Firefighter
SERVING 11/7/1994 SINCE

Javier Hernandez
Firefighter

SERVING 11/10/2003 SINCE

Andrew Holtfreter
Firefighter

SERVING 5/07/2007 SINCE

Nathan Hughes
Firefighter

SERVING 11/21/2005 SINCE

Ted Hyde
Firefighter

SERVING 2/17/2004 SINCE

Daniel Jordan
Firefighter

SERVING 11/7/1994 SINCE

John Keelan
Firefighter

SERVING 5/22/1978 SINCE

Gary Lehmann
Firefighter

SERVING 7/19/1982 SINCE

Mitchell Li
Firefighter

SERVING 4/30/2007 SINCE

Anthony Liddell
Firefighter

SERVING 2/27/1989 SINCE

Michael Maalouf
Firefighter

SERVING 8/29/2005 SINCE

John Manos
Firefighter

SERVING 4/15/2002 SINCE

Lori Marchetti
Firefighter

SERVING 6/19/2006 SINCE

James Marold
Firefighter

SERVING 6/17/2002 SINCE

Mark McCann
Firefighter

SERVING 6/17/2002 SINCE

Daniel McCarry
Firefighter

SERVING 1/3/1977 SINCE

Jose Mendia
Firefighter

SERVING 11/25/2002 SINCE

Amy Mertes
Firefighter

SERVING 11/21/2005 SINCE

Matthew Milone
Firefighter

SERVING 7/1/2002 SINCE

Kenneth Miranda
Firefighter
SERVING 5/10/1993 SINCE

Abiud Montes
Firefighter
SERVING 12/12/1994 SINCE

Robert Montgomery
Firefighter
SERVING 4/15/2002 SINCE

Andrew Mossop
Firefighter
SERVING 1/3/1989 SINCE

James Mott
Firefighter
SERVING 2/5/1980 SINCE

Andrew Nelson
Firefighter
SERVING 1/3/1989 SINCE

Hugh O'Donnell
Firefighter
SERVING 11/21/2005 SINCE

Dennis O'Toole
Firefighter
SERVING 5/27/1986 SINCE

Henry Olmetti
Firefighter
SERVING 2/27/1984 SINCE

Shana Pender
Firefighter

SERVING 3/11/2002 SINCE

Rita Pereira
Firefighter

SERVING 5/07/2007 SINCE

Daniel Pittard
Firefighter

SERVING 12/4/1995 SINCE

Christopher Plummer
Firefighter

SERVING 9/18/1995 SINCE

Tim Poole
Firefighter

SERVING 9/16/2002 SINCE

Kevin Quinn
Firefighter

SERVING 10/2/1989 SINCE

Jerrel Ray II
Firefighter

SERVING 9/18/1995 SINCE

Kevin Reekie
Firefighter

SERVING 11/19/2001 SINCE

Travis Rienhart
Firefighter

SERVING 12/10/2007 SINCE

Daryel Richards
Firefighter
SERVING | 6/3/1996 | SINCE

Jon Rieschl
Firefighter
SERVING | 1/12/1998 | SINCE

Klaus Rose
Firefighter
SERVING | 12/10/2007 | SINCE

James Russo
Firefighter
SERVING | 2/26/1996 | SINCE

Michael Saffran
Firefighter
SERVING | 5/07/2007 | SINCE

Armando Sanchez
Firefighter
SERVING | 11/21/2005 | SINCE

Jack Saunders
Firefighter
SERVING | 12/15/1997 | SINCE

Holly Schmorr
Firefighter
SERVING | 5/31/2005 | SINCE

Amy Schwarz
Firefighter
SERVING | 11/21/2005 | SINCE

Simon Serrao
Firefighter
SERVING | 5/9/2005 | SINCE

Jason Simione
Firefighter
SERVING | 9/18/1995 | SINCE

Henry Steinbuck
Firefighter
SERVING | 1/3/1989 | SINCE

Christopher Sullivan
Firefighter
SERVING | 3/8/2004 | SINCE

Cindy Taffel
Firefighter
SERVING | 12/10/2007 | SINCE

Richard Taylor
Firefighter
SERVING | 7/20/1987 | SINCE

Marcy Treadwell
Firefighter
SERVING | 11/10/2003 | SINCE

Adam Ura
Firefighter
SERVING | 11/10/2003 | SINCE

Anthony Vera
Firefighter
SERVING | 1/12/1998 | SINCE

Jeffrey Vidal
Firefighter
SERVING | 8/29/2005 | SINCE

Anthony Vinas
Firefighter
SERVING | 05/19/1997 | SINCE

Raymond Wagner
Firefighter
SERVING | 6/29/1998 | SINCE

Jeffrey Webb
Firefighter
SERVING | 5/30/1977 | SINCE

Josh Wells
Firefighter
SERVING | 8/29/2005 | SINCE

Brian Wilkie
Firefighter
SERVING | 12/6/2004 | SINCE

Patrick Wilkie
Firefighter
SERVING | 1/10/2005 | SINCE

Adrian Wong
Firefighter
SERVING | 11/21/2005 | SINCE

Jameel Ziadie
Firefighter
SERVING | 4/15/2002 | SINCE

Rudy Kuchenberg and Bob Aspinall practice lowering an injured firefighter (classmate John Kebler)

Station 40, "The Rock"

Firefighter Jack Bealmear takes a moment to catch his breath after a fire.

Antique American LaFrance fire engine, circa 1920

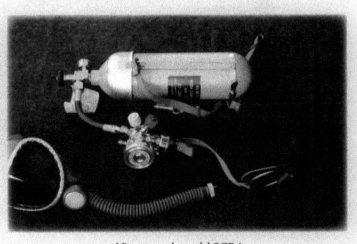

Vintage early model SCBA

Hollywood Fire College, circa 1970

1925 American LaFrance

Trainees learn how to bring an unconscious man down the ladder

Rob Hazen hams it up for the camera during rope drills

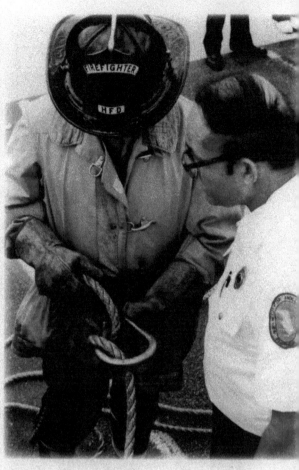

Training Officer Tony Muniz explains how to prepare a safety line

Firefighter Chris Boyle at an apartment fire ('82)

Fully Involved!

A firefighter tests his new air pack

Heat Mirage

Antique ladder truck

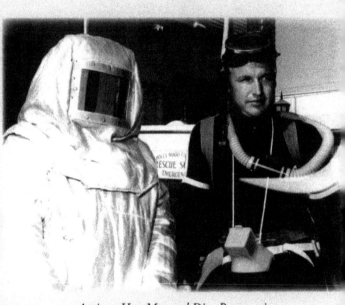

Antique Haz-Mat and Dive Rescue suits

Scott Bazy & Joe Eutsey at Station 31

Engine 3 cab

Fire Chief Holloway L. Cook and Command Staff

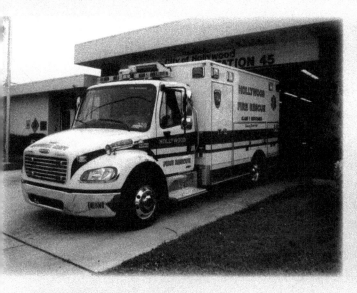

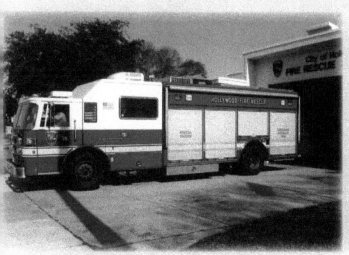

911 Call Center/Dispatch

Emergency Operation Center

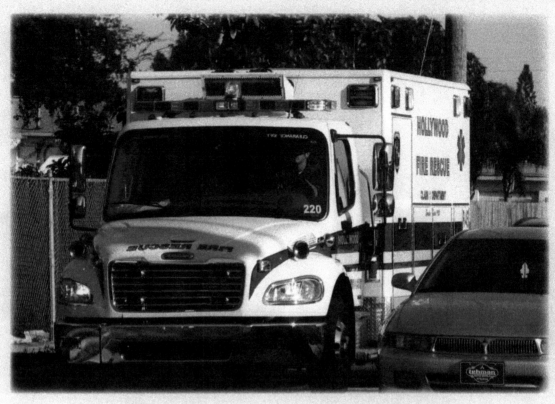

Lieutenant John Kebler and Firefighter Ralph Fuentes on Rescue 45

Driver Engineer Lamar Davis connects to the pumper

Driver Engineer Kenneth Cressler at a Technical Rescue Drill

Firefighter Brian Wilkie, Captain Morris James, and Driver Engineer Charles Redding rush to the scene of an accident

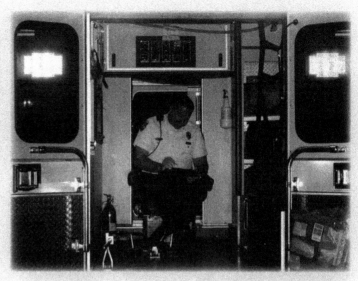

Lieutenant Mike Briosi gets ready to take a patient's information

Lieutenant Tom Karl (ret.) sets a knot for rope rescue training with Lieutenant Joe Gambino

Lieutenant Mike Fulks, Captain Chris Pratt & Firefighter Rick Harvey finish another call in District 5

Firefighter Dan McCarry and Driver Engineer Mark Ramsay exit a smoke-filled warehouse

Firefighter Jason Simione, Driver Engineer Brian White, Driver Engineer Joe Fisher, Driver Engineer Bill Jones, Firefighter Dean Eyerman, and Firefighters Bob Montgomery and George Burns after a Haz-Mat call

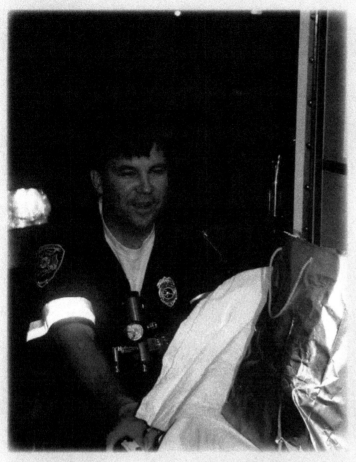

Firefighter Geza Hegedus loads up the stretcher

Firefighters George Burns and Dean Eyerman prep Rescue 31 after a call.

Driver Engineer Diana DeAbreu operating the pump panel

Forced entry at a structure fire

You can always count on Rescue Captain Dave Danko for on scene help

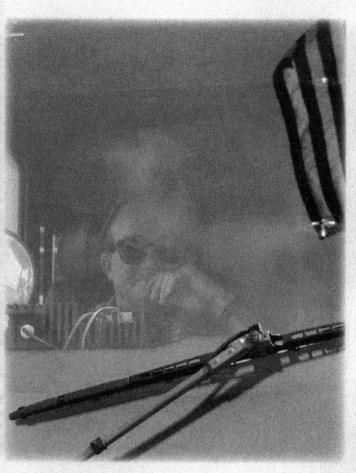

Driver Engineer Paul Watson tries to escape the heat in the Captain's seat

Matt Phillips at the "Big One"

Firefighter Joe Amy loading a patient

Firefighters Dan Dapolito and Bill Biglin

Captain Kenneth Delbert, always there for the little ones

Captain Dan Fitzgerald preparing to respond to a call

Fire's out

Marine Safety Officer Andrea Cross checks out a potential problem on the beach

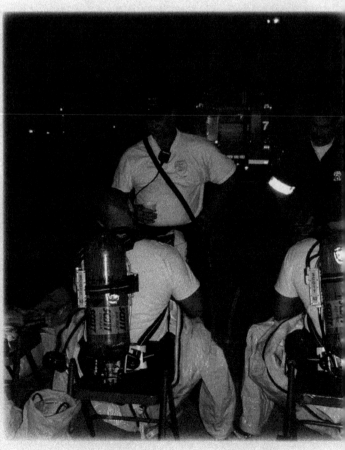

Haz-Mat team at work in Hallandale

Fire Chief Virgil Fernandez and Lieutenant Larry Allwine talk Haz-Mat

Lieutenant Marc Croteau logging rehab info

Decon at a Haz-Mat call

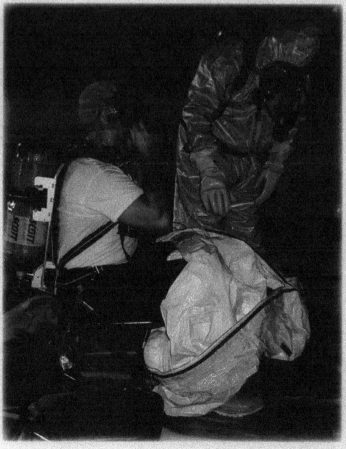

Time for rehab

Probationary Firefighters Derek Avilez, Rocio Cervini, Jose Fernandez, Mike Gulla, Lori Marchetti, and Steven Zelenka catch their first fire while still in training

Driver Engineer Tom Karl (ret.), Firefighters George Burns, Dreu Mossop, Pat Wilkie, Brian White, and Chris Sullivan begin treating an injured driver

Firefighter Ray Wagner

Ron White makes the cut

Engine and Rescue crews respond to a 'truck vs. house'

Partial roof collapse at the Fashion Mall

Surround and drown

Defensive Ops

Guy Lanciault, Dave Knott, Don Anderson, Dan Jordan, Dave Sheldon, Bill Biglin, Bert Fernandez, Gary Skinner, Javier Hernandez, Joe Amy, and Kurt Ladwig wind down after the fire

Ladder Operations

After the fire

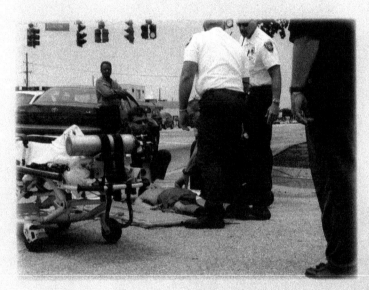

Firefighter Geza Hegedus, Firefighter Rick Harvey, Lieutenant Mike Fulks, and Rescue Captain Dave Danko treat a trauma victim on 441

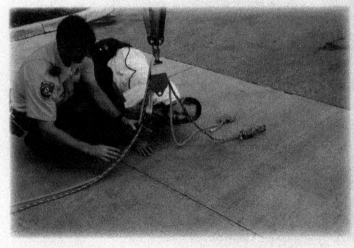

Driver Engineer Marc Croteau and Captain Mark Claxon inspect TRT rigging

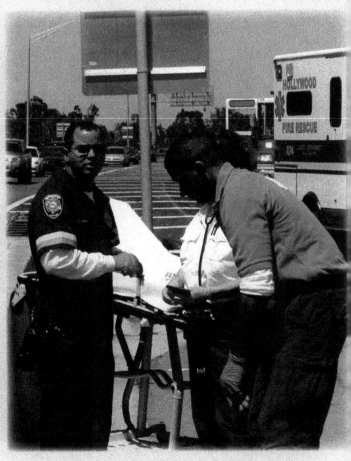

Firefighter Abiud Montes hard at work on I-95

Flammable Liquids training

Firefighters Joe Gambino, Kent Seamanson, and Joe Rohan check things out after a fire

Post incident discussion with Lieutenant Don Perdue (ret.), Assistant Chief George Giesler (ret.), Assistant Chief Wayne Malliard (ret.), and Battalion Chief Joe Rohan

Rookie Frank Wade waiting for water

A rollover in District 45

Captain Bob Munson (ret.), Battalion Chief Morris James, and Firefighters James Russo and Hank Olmetti on scene of an auto accident

Firefighters John Shelton and Bill Gutierrez with Captain Donald Dowell (ret.).

Firefighter Tony Vera is ready to go

Firefighters Frank Wade and Steve Newmark making sure the fire's out

HazMat hot zone

Lifeguard Fernando Marrero keeps a watchful eye on the beach

Car fire

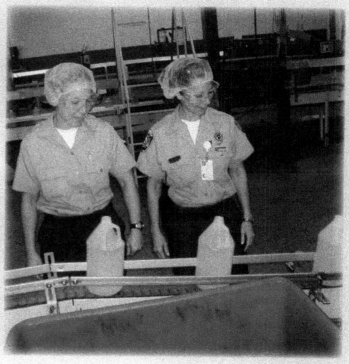

Recruit Lori Marchetti gets a lesson in Fire Code inspecting by Firefighter Dawn Clarke

Marine Safety Officer Rick Fiorillo and Marine Safety Chief Jim Shoemaker (ret.) enjoy a beautiful day on the beach

Loran "Corkey" Cochran investigates a fire

Pictured clockwise from bottom: Lieutenant Jim Toncos (ret.), Lieutenant Frank Meyer (ret.), Driver Engineer Joe Fisher, Driver Engineer Larry Allwine, Captain John Kusuk, Firefighter Chris Taylor, Firefighter Andrew Mossop, Firefighter Jason Simione, and Firefighter Dean Eyerman.

Firefighter Diana DeAbreu shows how much she loves her job

Training Officer Mark Steele and Battalion Chief Lamar Davis

Two peas in a pod Firefighters Pete Robinson and Gary Lehmann

Captain Pete Hanna (ret.) and Captain Claud Addicott (ret.) attend Open House

Lieutenant Rick Whippy (ret.) representing the Yesteryear Village Fire Department and Museum at an Open House

Driver Engineer John Kusuk and Captain Marty Cooper (ret.) catching up on paperwork at Station 5

Lifeguard Amy Schwarz with Firefighter Ron Mott

Firefighters Brian White and Rick Harvey show how we support each other during the work day

Battalion Chief Gary Peebles (ret.) in front of a vintage pumper

Lieutenant Mark Ellis looks on as Driver Engineer Mike Cardillo prepares dinner

Captain John Johnson enjoying a bowl of soup

Lieutenant Larry Latore, Lieutenant Chuck Johnson, and Driver Engineer Skip White

Firefighters Matt Milone and Richard Taylor take a load off

Battalion Chiefs Dave Danko and Morris James – a handsome pair

Driver Engineer John Kuklinski pours himself a cup of joe

So photogenic, FPO III Gary Sexsmith

Firefighter Marcus Fresco and Driver Engineer Jim Cummins enjoy the view

Lieutenant Frank Meyer (ret.) and pooch

Lieutenant Kevin Reardon and Firefighter Jorge Castano's smiling faces

Firefighters Dave Guernsey, Chris Sullivan, Dan Jordan and Kerry Boyett try to avoid dish pan hands

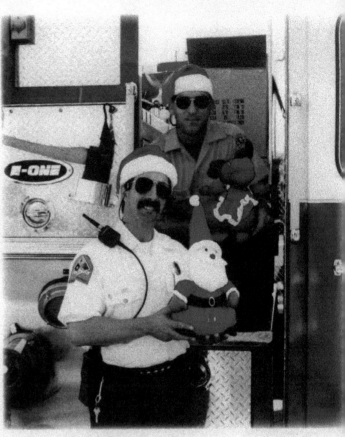

Lieutenant Joe Gambino and Driver Engineer Chuck Johnson (ret.) collect toys for "Toys for Tots"

Beach Safety's Captain Vince Canosa rolls in to Headquarters

Driver Engineer William Gutierrez happy to be in Battalion Chief Dave Danko's office and out of trouble

Fire Marshal Bob Madge (ret.) gets ready to give a talk on fire safety

Battalion Chief Charlie Barbera enjoying a holiday meal

Driver Engineer David Knott and Firefighter John Wenth goof around

FPO II Rob Hazen and FPO III Bill Kay (ret.) get ready to go to court

Captain Lou Carman taking it easy at Station 31

Training Officer Wayne Bruce (ret.) explains how to raise the Bangor Ladder to Firefighters Rob Hazen, Rudy Kuchenberg (ret.), Bob Aspinall and other members of their training class.

Driver Engineer Tom Price keeps a close eye on the turkey

Lieutenant Larry Allwine organizes a special dinner celebrating the en of Hurricane Wilma in 2005

Kevin Dodds prepares his rookie dinner

Jack Saunders keeps his word and only cuts his hair after Herb Helfe returned to work

Driver Engineer Tom Price, Firefighter Holly Schmorr, and Captain Dan Fitzgerald make a great crew

Driver Engineer Mark Miller and Firefighter Dawn Clarke can still manage a smile while working hard to feed the masses at Station 74

Lieutenant Rick Arndt diving in

Firefighter Ken Miranda, Captain Tom Dingus, Battalion Chief Mark Steele, Firefighter Bob Montgomery, & Captain Dave Swick hand out flowers in honor of Mother's Day at Open House

Driver Engineer Herbie Helfen making dinner at Station 40.

Firefighters Phil Edelman and Mark McCann enjoy a Station 5 feast.

Driver Engineer Dave Civita is ready to roll!

Firefighter Dave Guernsey, Firefighter Chris Sullivan, Driver Engineer Bill Biglin, Firefighter Humberto Fernandez, and Firefighter Javier Hernandez at Station 5

Lieutenant Kevin Politte, Firefighter John Manos, and Firefighter Marc Treadwell snacking at Station 74

Captain John Bridenburg's rippling forearms prove he can handle the Department's newly issued helmets.

Firefighters Andrew Estevez and Pat Wilkie enjoy a rare quiet moment at Station 5, while Firefighter Kevin Reekie applies the second coat.

Captain Charles Colson looking his most aerodynamic.

Dispatcher Andrew Estevez in his past life.

Promotions! Division Chief Joe Gambino, Battalion Chief Gary Smith, and Battalion Chief Mark Steele with new Lieutenants Rudy Jurado, Kurt Ladwig, David Selby, new Driver Engineers Diana DeAbreu, Juan Lana, Chuck Tullio, Eric Guerrero, Training Instructor Jorge Castano, and FPO II Janet Washburn.

Joe Gambino, Charlie Barbera, Joe Rohan, & Mark Steele serve up lunch to hungry City of Hollywood employees

Kerry Boyett, Kevin Dodds, Dan Dapolito, Joe Gambino, Brian White, Joe Fisher, Phil Edelman, Jeff Vidal, Jeff Davidson, Chuck Colson, Steve Newmark, and Morris James share an award on the steps of City Hall

Firefighters Hank Olnetti & Dan Pittard investigate the mysteries of the photocopier

Captain Bill Major, Firefighter Diana DeAbreu, and Lt. Chris Korn exchanging District 5 stories.

Driver Engineer Tommy Karl's last supper

Driver Engineer Dave Civita operates the Platform

*Fire Chief Virgil Fernandez congratulating newly promoted Driv
Engineer Juan Lana*

Lieutenant Gary Smith looks on during an aerial training exercise

Driver Engineer Charlie Redding mans the controls of Platform 5

Recruits Marcy Hofle, Javier Hernandez, Phil Edelman, Chris Clinton, and Adam Ura face the dreaded geography test

Firefighter Mark Cowart, Driver Enginer John Kuklinski, and Captain Scott Bazy with Santa

Firefighter Kurt Ladwig taking a breather

Firefighters Alex Poli and Diana DeAbreu assaulting the beach at TY Park during dive training.

Captain Larry Latore and Driver Engineer Jack Bealmear show TV personality Belkys Nerey some Hollywood hospitality.

Firefighters Al Burchardt and Mike Fulks respond to a rescue call

Firefighter Joe Amy, Driver Engineer Kenny Miranda, and Firefighter Phil Edelman share a few quiet moments after lunch

Captain Don Dowell (ret.) at T.Y. Park

Driver Engineer Steve Reese thinks lunch is the best part of his day!

Fire Chief Virgil Fernandez and Lisa Blouin join forces to do some housekeeping

Lieutenant Mark Miller, Firefighter Henry Steinbuck, and Firefighter Kevin Dodds stop by Station 74

Firefighter Derek Avilez checks the PASS Device on a Scott Tank

Driver Engineer Al Wasserman, Lieutenant Ron White, and Captain Ray Powers practice their rope rappelling techniques

Battalion Chief Gary Smith, Division Chief Robert Aspinall, Division Chief Lamar Davis, Division Chief Joe Gambino, and Battalion Chief Mark Steele join Fire Chief Virgil Fernandez and Deputy Fire Chief Joe Rohan in congratulating Tony Liddell on being named Firefighter of the Year for 2005

Firefighter Mike O'Donnell cooks up a feast for the masses

Tony Vera, Ron White, Juan Lana, Chuck Colson, Mark McCann, Pat Moore, & Chris Sullivan smile for the camera at the annual Public Service Recognition Week "Lunch on the Lawn"

Division Chief Robert Aspinall, and Deputy Fire Chief Joseph Rohan welcome the Department's Chaplains; Father Rodger Holoubek and Reverend Garland Robertson

Firefighter Ted Hyde helps Administrative Assistant II Beve. Busenbarrick (ret.) and Administrative Assistant Pat Hall to their fi platform ride while Captain Ray Powers and Firefighter Ron Mott g: a much needed pep talk

Firefighter Rocio Cervini gets started on those ever-present station duties

Beach Safety personnel complete their morning workout

SPECIAL EVENT PHOTOS

Firefighters Daniel McCarry, Mike Cardillo, and Jose Mendia at the annual Saint Patrick's Day Parade in New York City

Firefighter Henry Steinbuck and Lieutenant Al Burchardt in line for chow at the annual Public Service Employee Recognition Week Luncheon

Deputy Fire Chief Joe Rohan and Division Chief Bob Aspinall join Division Chief Charlie Barbera as he accepts the coveted Silver Spoon Award which is awarded to the best server at the annual Public Service Employee Recognition Week Luncheon

Firefighters Abby Montes, Eric Guerrero, John Kellerman, & Tony Vinas present the colors for the opening of Station 74

Firefighters Janet Washburn and Marlene Harden ham it up during the Station 74 Ribbon Cutting ceremony

Bonnie Hogue, Donna D'Angelo, Lisa Blouin, Janet Gurdyal, Kim Graves, & Barbara Greenfield attend the ribbon cutting for Station 74

The Mayor & Commissioners "Cut" the Ribbon for Station 74 ceremony

Medical Director Dr. Richard Dellerson and Battalion Chief Lamar Davis smile for the camera during the opening of Station 74

Jack Downs (ret.) and wife Judy attend the opening of Station 74

Training Officers Mark Steele and Wayne Bruce (ret.) at the Station 74 Ribbon Cutting

Battalion Chief Jack McMillan (ret.) and Training Officer Dan Blundy discuss the attributes of the newly christened Fire Station 74

Battalion Chief Don Dowell (ret.) and Battalion Chief Bob Aspinall talk shop during the Station 74 Ribbon Cutting ceremony

Freckles the Fire Dog at an Open House

Training Officer Lamar Davis giving a demonstration at Open House

Herminio Lorenzo, Fire Chief ('94-'99), next to Platform 5

Clowning around at an Open House

Crash Test Dummies working the crowd

Battalion Chief Jim Johnson (ret.) enjoying one of his favorite activities, supervising the hydrant painting at an Open House

Lieutenant Tom Karl (ret.) and family at an Open House

Deputy Fire Chief Wayne Malliard (ret.) grabs some lunch at an Open House

Driver Engineer Larry Allwine putting out flames at Open House

Hollywood's finest: Dawn Clarke, Shana Pender, and Marcy Treadwell

Chris Taylor and Mark Miller with little ones.

City of Miami's vintage Ladder Truck 1/3 at an open house

Live burn!

135

Joe DiMaggio Children's Hospital Helicopter makes an appearance at the '06 Open House

Brian White with brother and crash test dummy Ron White

Kevin Dodds back in his Explorer days demonstrates how to handle hose

Hollywood's most comical Driver Engineer

Battalion Chief Lamar Davis goes over LifePak operations

Gary Sexsmith and Gary Smith with their grandchildren

Dan Pittard and Holly Schmorr pose for the camera with a tiny future firefighter

Battalion Chief Bob Aspinall, Division Chief Norman Mahalsky (ret.) Fire Chief Randall Burrough ('99-'02)

Driver Engineer Kenny Cressler helping a youngster donn bunker gear

Lieutenant Bob Buckner (ret.) putting a mask on a willing volunteer

Lieutenant Joe Gambino, Driver Engineer Bill Jones, and Driver Engineer Gary Skinner get ready to demonstrate a vehicle extrication at an Open House

Extrication Demonstration at Station 74 during Open House.

Extrication complete!

Saved another one

Hazmat Drill

Mark Claxon and John Kusuk with Chuckles the Clown

Former Fire Chiefs Jim Ward ('82-'94) and Randall Burrough ('99-'02) with former Asst. Chief George Geisler.

Firefighters Stephen Ciorrocco and Ron Mott, Captain Joe Stolarz and Driver Engineer Mike Briosi having a good time at the annual Christmas party

Captain Morris James and his wife, Desiree, enjoying the 2003 Recognition Banquet

Dave Guernsey and fiance, Kelly, take time out of their salad course for a photo at the 2003 Banquet.

Department retirees take a group photo at the '05 Banquet Front Row: Jac Dunlap, Rich Brito, Dick Brown, Jim Ward, Bill Savery. Middle Row: Ed Tarmey (Dania Fire), Gary Peebles, Charlie Isbill, Rick Whippy, Don Dowell. Back Row: Lloyd Holden (Dania Fire), Bobby Hay, Rudy Kuchenberg, Larry Manion, Bob Kimmich (Dania Fire), Jim Toncos, Bob Madge, Randy Burrough, Paul Comeau, Bob Allen.

Fire Chief Virgil Fernandez presents retiree Jim Toncos with his bugle at the '05 Banquet.

Don Dowell gives a short speech after being honored at the '05 Banque

Jac Dunlap happily takes his bugle from Chief Fernandez at the '05 Banquet

Eric Busenbarrick & Dan Fitzgerald present Russ Chard with a speci award at the '05 Banquet

Tanya Bouloy and Jeff Davidson present awards at the '06 Banquet

Brian Ettinger, Amy Schwarz, Nate Hughes, and Armando Sanchez show how well they clean up at the '06 Banquet

Rick Pingol, Morris James, Dave Danko, Diana DeAbreu, Bob Aspinall, Virgil Fernandez, Joe Gambino, and Jeff Davidson at the '06 Banquet

2006 Banquet Honorees Dick Russell, Don Anderson, Willie Conner, Pete Hanna, Tom Karl, Bill Klitch, Steve Luongo, Jack McMillan, & Gar Peebles proudly accept their bugles from Fire Chief Virgil Fernandez

UNION HISTORY

In 1960, twenty-six members of the fire department took the name of "The Hollywood Fire Fighters" and received their union charter as Local #1375 of the International Association of Fire Fighters. They were pioneers in a career service that was not yet receptive to labor unions.

In the early years, the Union functioned as little more than a fraternal organization; there were no labor laws that compelled the city to recognize it as a representative of the firefighters. When wage increases or other benefit changes were desired by the members, the Union would approach the City manager with a "Wish List" of requests for his consideration. More often than not, the City Manager would say "Thanks, but no thanks." Due to political and community pressures (and perhaps sensing the inevitable), the City Manager finally conceded voluntary recognition of the Union in 1973 and the first collective bargaining agreement became effective on March 6, 1974.

The Union has almost always held membership in the statewide firefighter association. Originally known as "The Professional Fire Fighters of Florida," it changed its name to "The Florida Professional Firefighters" during the 1980's (the Union became known as "The Hollywood Professional Fire Fighters at the same time) in order to distinguish itself from volunteer firefighter groups. The success of this organization, in conjunction with other public employee unions (police, teachers, general employees, etc.) finally brought about legislative change in the mid-1970's. The State of Florida created the "Public Employees Relations Commission (P.E.R.C.)" and enacted a full chapter of state statutes to govern the processes of collective bargaining, grievances, impasse resolutions, unfair labor practices, and much more. From the Union's perspective, it was a welcomed improvement but it still left several deficiencies in the law, most of which remain to this day (i.e. no binding arbitration or right-to-strike).

Entering the 1970's, Hollywood was fairly well paid by fire department standards. Then the recession hit and Hollywood fell far behind area standards for wages and benefits. By the late 1970's, the situation had gotten so bad that the Union was able to secure exemptions from applicable federal wage controls and was granted two-year wage increases totaling 18%.

In September of 1980, the members of the police and fire departments participated in a "Blue Flu" that was to become one of the most infamous events in the history of Florida public sector labor law. It is referenced in P.E.R.C. manuals and writings to this day.

During the 1980's the public began to view labor

Left: The current Union Executive Board: (l to r) Chuck Tullio, Dan Martinez, Diana DeAbreu, Russ Chard, Dave Duensing, Eric Busenbarrick, John Kuklinski and Lou Carman.

Rendering of the future Union Hall

organizations in a different way. Aggressive, confrontational and "strong-arm" tactics that were solidly supported during the 1970's fell out of favor. The work force was shifting from "blue" to "white-collar" employees and public sentiment reflected it. In order to remain effective, the Union needed to modify its methods. Dramatic changes in the political environment led to a positive effect on the manner in which the Fire Administration, the City, and the Union approached labor relations. Today, the parties resolve most issues as partners instead of as opponents. Agreements are publicly highlighted and conflicts are minimized so as to negate their impact in non-related areas. Circumstances have finally allowed labor relations to become a mutually beneficial business instead of a battleground.

During the forty-eight years in which these changes occurred, eleven firefighters have served as Union President. John Coyne was the first and went on to become Fire Chief as well. He was succeeded by Walter Battaglia and George Geisler, both of whom still retain the status of honorary members in the Local. Charlie Lenox was next, followed by Steve Cuthbert. Al Gilbert (a.k.a "The Flamingo") was the next president, even though he is best remembered for his many years in the office of Union Treasurer. He was followed by Don Anderson, who faced arrest as president during the events surrounding the "Blue Flu." Doug Macready served on Anderson's executive board and succeeded him in the office of president. Macready held the office until his death from leukemia on May 8, 1985. The union hall was re-dedicated as "Douglas B. Macready Hall" exactly one year later. Leon Davis took over upon Macready's death and served for approximately fifteen months. He was replaced by Don Barfield, who held the position for just over four years. In 1990, Barfield was followed by Russ Chard, who has, to date, served eighteen consecutive years in the position.

In recognition of their service, the following leaders have been awarded emeritus status within the Local: John Coyne and Doug Macready, President Emeritus; Don Barfield, Vice President Emeritus; and Al Gilbert, Treasurer Emeritus.

Although these men have served in leadership roles, it remains the rank and file membership that makes a union strong. The Union's strength and unity has defined the Local and has enabled it to survive and excel through some of the most chaotic periods experienced by any public labor organization in the state.

THE BLUE FLU

During the summer of 1980, all three labor unions in the City of Hollywood had undergone contract negotiations to no

avail. Trying to divide and conquer, the City had played one union against the other while claiming that there were insufficient dollars in the budget to satisfy the needs of all three groups. If the 1980-81 budget was finalized without any money set aside in contingency funds, the unions knew that it would be an unacceptably lean year at the bargaining table. Something needed to be done to draw attention to the situation.

On September 13, 1980, the police and fire department personnel in Hollywood experienced one of the most remarkable events in the history of Florida public sector labor law. That morning, public safety personnel were stricken with a mysterious illness that forced entire shifts of workers to call in sick to work. With reference to uniform color, the epidemic became known as the "Blue Flu." In response, the City was forced to hire workforces of overtime personnel in such numbers that there were actually more people on duty during this period than on normal work days. At no time were any citizens ever placed at risk. The illnesses continued for three days with a total of 104 firefighters calling in sick. During that time, Union President Don Anderson was consistently threatened with arrest for allegedly violating state law and initiating an illegal strike.

On the morning of September 16, the "flu bug" had apparently passed. Over 80 fire department personnel assembled a few blocks from the old Station #1 (now Station #5) and marched down the street to report for line-up at 0800 hours. A fraction of the marchers were actually scheduled to report for duty while the others went along to show their support.

At the final budget meeting, the Hollywood City Commission faced a standing-room-only crowd of City employees, their families and friends overflowing the commission chambers and spilling into the lobby and parking lots below. After hours of deliberation, the commission finally decided to grant two-year wage increases totaling 26.5% to all city employees.

Despite those positive results, neither the City nor the State of Florida took matters lightly. The Union continues to officially deny having participated in an illegal strike. However, the Public Employees Relations Commission found the Union guilty of orchestrating a "job action" and levied penalties: $12,500 fine paid by the Union and "sick" members had to donate forty-eight hours of unpaid time back to the City.

On July 1, 1982, The Union made its first $5,000 payment of the P.E.R.C. fine. Union President Doug Macready led a procession of 20 firefighters into the commission chamber where they filled a barrel full if 180,000 nickels and dimes. Panicked commissioners feared that the weight of the coins would break through the floor and crash into the work area below.

To this day, it remains the only strike/job action in the history of Florida public sector labor. The penalties got paid but all city employees continue to enjoy the benefits gained as a result of the "Blue Flu."

The Hollywood Firefighters' Pension Fund was created in 1955 and initially funded by member contributions, fire extinguisher servicing for the public and private sectors, and the sale of dance tickets to a "Guy Lombardi Band" event.

The Pension Plan was chartered by the State of Florida as a "Defined Benefit Plan" in 1963. The City then began to subsidize the Plan, and firefighters paid a contribution to receive a normal retirement benefit at age 55.

The first meeting of the Board of Trustees was held on April 25, 1964, with Mayor Bill Zinkil, Chief Holloway Cook, Trustees Bill Bell, Ed Guillod, Joe Muscarella and John Coyne; then the Union President, in attendance. John Coyne was very instrumental in organizing the Board.

Since that time, the Plan has undergone numerous benefit changes. One significant change occurred in 1989 when the Hollywood Firefighters' Pension Fund introduced the first Deferred Retirement Option Plan (D.R.O.P.) in the State of Florida. Other significant changes include a reduction in the number of years of employment or age before members are eligible for retirement.

With the exception of the mayor serving as chair of the board, members of the Pension Board include a city appointed chair, the Fire Chief who serves as the vice-chair, three elected firefighters, an administrator and one Administrative Assistant. Current Board members are:

Chair - Mr. Mark Butler
Vice Chair – Fire Chief Virgil Fernandez
Secretary – Chris Pratt
Trustee – Gary Ethridge
Trustee – William Huddleston
Administrator – Rich Brito
Administrative Assistant – Patricia Hall

Rich Brito
Fund Administrator

Pat Hall
Administrative Assistant

PensionBoard: (Seated) Trustee, Gary Ethridge, Chair, Mark Butler, Administrative Assistant, Pat Hall, Secretary, Chris Pratt (Standing) Stephen Cypen, Vice Chair, Virgil Fernandez, Administrator, Rich Brito, Trustee, Bill Huddleston

Retirement, the word no longer brings to mind pictures of spending your days quietly in the garden and occasionally visiting the grandchildren. Today's retirees often find themselves busier than when they worked full time, only now its time spent doing the things that are most fulfilling.

Aside from traveling between his home in South Florida and cabin in the Georgia Mountains Jim Johnson volunteers for the Red Cross. His involvement with the Red Cross found him giving relief assistance in Mississippi for three weeks after Hurricane Katrina devastated the area in 2005. Jim also volunteers for various department functions.

Bill Sabino, who currently resides in Virginia, spends his time fulfilling his childhood dream of making a living as an artist.

Jim Ward and his wife Kathy spend their time with family, traveling and fishing. They continue to make their primary home the Florida Keys and find that retirement is indeed wonderful.

Rick Whippy spends time as a member of The Asphalt Angels, an antique car show group. He and Peggy also spend their time traveling, fishing, and spending valuable time with their growing family.

The ever energetic Hutch Clark can still be occasionally found in the hallways of Fire Administration where she helps to keep the staff going with her cakes and has a made a significant contribution to the Department's newly create photo archive.

Don & Kathy Dowell, when not sprucing up their 3 acre farm in Tennessee, have become quite the globe trotter Poland, Russia, Italy, Greece and various stops in the US a just a few of their trips since Don's last day. Don and Kathy a living their dream of traveling the world.

Dick Russell lives out his dream of spending his da fishing and continues to enter competitions as well as ju fishing for the sport of it.

Ever wonder where Christmas trees come from? Ask B and Donna Conner. They have dedicated part of their 9 acre New Hampshire farm to growing Christmas trees. Whe not brush hogging or gathering eggs from their chickens th enjoy their days snowmobiling, ice fishing, and skiing. B also spends time fishing, hunting and black smithing.

From traveling to competitive fishing, to showing antiq cars to working as an artist, to being a disaster relief work to continued involvement with the department it all mak it clear to see that our retirees have a myriad of activities a interests to keep them busy!

Fred Lunsford, Bill Savery, Rick Whippy, George Geisler, Randy Burrough, Jim Toncos, Don Barfield, Dave Frohock

Walter Battaglia, Dan Damiano, Ralph Curtis, Paul Comeau, R Brito, Jack Wilson, Marty Hodos, Ralph Renn, Joe Muscarella

Fred Fisher, Jack Downs, John Preece, Wayne Barnes, Don Anderson, Jim Wright, Charlie Bouck

Ted Ferschke, Tom Karl, Bill Clark, Pete Hanna

New retiree Beverly Busenbarrick poses with 4 of her 5 Fire Chiefs: Virgil Fernandez, Jim Ward ('82-'94), Randall Burrough ('99-'02) and Herminio Lorenzo ('94-'99)

Don & Kathy Dowell enjoy off roading on their Lutts, Tennessee property

Hutch Clark kicks up her heels at the 2006 Recognition Banquet with fellow retiree Don Anderson

Ted & Pauline Ferschke enjoy a dinner and dance

Bill & Donna Conner take a time out from their Christmas trees

Jim and Connie Johnson take a moment out of their busy travel schedule to pose for this picture

Rick & Peggy Whippy take a moment to show off their 1970 Chevy Pickup at a car show

Jeff Salerno, Dave Salerno & Dick Russell show off their latest dolphi catch

Jim Ward pulling in a good size sailfish on one of his fishing trips

Attendees at the June 2006 HFRA meeting laugh at one of Rich's usu jokes

Lucile Ornawka and Joyce Hofacker attend a Retiree's Association Meeting

George Geisler, Pat Hall, and Rich Brito preside over a HFRA meeti

The Benevolent Board:
(L to R) Kevin Quinn, Bill Huddleston, Frank Wade, John Bridenburg, and Pete Falk

Hollywood Firefighter's Benevolent Association

The Hollywood Firefighter's Benevolent Association was formed in the early to mid-1950's in support of the welfare and benefit of all department members. A separate entity from the Union, it is governed by a Board of Directors who decide how Benevolent funds are allocated.

In earlier years, the Benevolent Association funded the purchase of daily newspapers, flowers for deceased family members of department personnel, gym equipment and donations to charitable organizations. Revenue was generated from soda vending machines placed in the fire stations, annual Christmas tree sales and from unsolicited private donations.

The Benevolent Association currently provides financial support for the annual Firefighters' Picnic, entry fees for members participating in the annual Firefighter Olympics and other member-related benefits.

Following the sudden death of Driver/Engineer Tom Park in 1982, the Benevolent Association established the Tom Park Scholarship Fund after receiving numerous donations in his honor. The Benevolent Board of Directors established criteria for a scholarship program and annually selects a recipient from the Department's Fire Explorer Post.

The success of the Hollywood Firefighter's Benevolent Association is the result of commitment, hard work and dedication by its board members, past and present. With the service of the board members and the support of the membership, the Benevolent will continue to foster goodwill throughout the ranks, helping to establish a feeling of family.

Mel Manion has a smile for the camera at the annual benevolent picnic

Bill Clark, Ted Ferschke, and Bill Savery, "The Over the Hill Gang," hang out at the picnic

Tanya Bouloy steps out from behind the camera to enjoy the picnic

As the DJ plays "You're so vain," Art Meadows watches as Morris James gets his groove on

Phil Edelman, Pat Moore, Courtney Fitzgerald, Chris Sullivan, Joel Medina, and Garrett Medina

Jim Russo, Dan Pittard, Daryel Richards, and James Richards at the 2008 Picnic

In The Line Of Duty Deaths

Gilbert J. Higgins
George McCall
James F. Woodruff
Loran "Corky" Cochran

Tuesday Morning, September 11, 2001

The whole world reacted as one, first with surprise and then with shock as the World Trade Center (WTC) in New York became the target of the worst terrorist attack ever unleashed anywhere on the planet, let alone on American soil. But even the most stunned observers took comfort in knowing that America's first line of defense, the men and women of the fire service, were hard at work evacuating civilians and preparing to attack the duplicate infernos.

Then the unimaginable happened.

Shock became horror as first the North Tower and then the South Tower of the WTC crumbled into a massive pile of twisted steel and shattered concrete. The twin tributes to American engineering and commerce had been replaced by a mountain of rubble and blanket of concrete dust that literally suffocated lower Manhattan.

While most of the world asked itself "How many civilians had managed to get out?" everyone associated with emergency fire/rescue services asked themselves "How many firefighters had managed to work their way in?" They immediately realized that this was to be the deadliest day in the history of professional firefighting.

It would be weeks before the full scope of the tragedy could be measured. Ultimately, the International Association of Fire Fighters (IAFF) recognized 347 (343 FDNY, 1 New York City Fire Patrol, 3 World Trade Center Fire Directors) Line of Duty deaths associated with the events of that tragic day. From coast to coast, Americans cried with the same voice, wept the same tears, and bonded together like no other time since World War II. When it was over, they had embraced the men and women of the fire service like never before. Firefighters became universally revered as "America's Heroes", finally achieving a level of recognition and appreciation that had often been overlooked.

Along with the emotional outpouring, America took step to ensure that those firefighters who had sacrificed their lives t protect others would now have their own families protected. I thousands of cities across America, fellow firefighters took t the streets for the largest fund raising "boot drive" in history In Hollywood alone, over $150,000 was raised through th generosity of the public, helping to increase the national tot into the hundreds of millions. The donations were channele through the IAFF to ensure that the surviving family member would be financially secure, including guaranteed colleg tuitions for their children.

One year later, over 5,000 members of the fire/rescu service from all over the world congregated in Colorado Spring Colorado, to pay tribute as their fallen brethren were honore during the annual ceremony at the IAFF Fallen Firefighte Memorial. Members of each affected family were guests at th service, had their loved ones individually recognized, and wer presented with an encased American flag in memory of thei loss and sacrifice.

While America must always remember those firefighte who died at the World Trade Center, the IAFF realized tha the loss of any firefighter at any time is equally as tragic fo those who knew and loved them. Accordingly, in conjunctio with the fifth anniversary of the WTC attack, the delegates c the 48th Biennial Convention of the IAFF unanimously passe "Resolution 9/11" that resolves "…that 9/11 of each year b solemnly recognized as a Day of Remembrance for all fir fighters, who fall in the line of duty, everywhere."

We Shall Never Forget.

Russell R. Chard

Lets us never forget the tragic events of September 11, 2001

Throughout Manhattan flyers requesting information about missing persons were a common sight

Cruel Toll: 350 Comrades

Firefighter Losses

WORST U.S. FIRES IN TERMS OF FIREFIGHTERS KILLED

April 1947 27 killed following fires and ammonium nitrate explosions aboard two ships docked at Texas City, Tex.

Dec. 1910 21 killed at a stockyard and cold storage warehouse in Chicago.

July 1956 19 killed at the Shamrock Oil and Gas Corp. refinery in Sun Ray, Tex.

July 1953 15 killed in a wildfire in the Mendocino National Forest in California.

July 6, 1994 14 killed in a wildfire on South Canyon Mountain near Glenwood Springs, Colo.

Estimated number of —— 350 firefighters missing in Tuesday's attack in New York. It is more than double the entire annual fatalities for firemen nationwide since at least 1977.

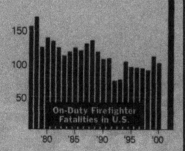

On-Duty Firefighter Fatalities in U.S.

'80 '95 '90 '95 '00

Sources: United States Fire Administration, FEMA; New York Fire Department; Associated Press

Firefighter Mike Cardillo passes by a number of vehicles totaled in the collapse of one of the towers

Firefighter Bill Biglin stops in front for a mangled FDNY engine

Helping firefighters' families

GIFT: A woman donates Friday to Hollywood firefighters for the New York Firefighters and Family Relief Fund at Sheridan Street and I-95. **Staff photo/ Michael Laughlin**

Hollywood Firefighters collect over $150,000 thanks to the generosity of the many citizens who donated to the effort

Local

Florida
BULLETIN BOARD
OBITUARIES
WEATHER

DA SUN-SENTINEL | WEDNESDAY | SEPTEMBER 19, 2001 | SECTION B

ATTACK ON AMERICA

Flying the flag high in Hollywood

PATRIOTISM UNFURLS: Firefighter Brian White unrolls a 20-by-12-foot American flag from the top of the water tower at Sheridan Street and Interstate 95 in Hollywood. White is a member of the city fire department's technical rescue team. **Staff photo/Lou Toman**

2B FRIDAY, SEPTEMBER 21, 2001 · NWS

ATTACK

Helping out

GIVING: Richard Singeltarry, 4, of Hollywood, donates to Capt. Steve Jones, of the Hollywood Fire Department, at Sheridan Street and Federal Highway on Thursday. The money helps the families of firefighters killed on Sept. 11. **Staff photo/Nam Y. Huh**

Battalion Chief Jack McMillan (ret.), Lieutenant Frank Meyer (ret.), Firefighter Dean Eyerman, Firefighter Eric Guerrero, Driver Engineer Willie Conner (ret.), Lieutenant Brian Cooke, & Firefighter Bi Gutierrez pitch in to help support the families of fallen firefighters

The Commemorative Book Committee consisted of:

Battalion Chief Morris James

Captain Scott Bazy

Captain Norman Rechtman

Driver Engineer Diana DeAbreu

Firefighter Fighter Jeff Vidal

Firefighter Holly Schmorr

Administrative Secretary Tanya Bouloy

Battalion Chief Morris James and Driver Engineer Diana DeAbreu review book sales

Firefighter Holly Schmorr and Administrative Secretary Tanya Bouloy review a small percentage of the thousands of pictures that were submitted for consideration

Captain Scott Bazy stops by "the yearbook office" to drop off sales forms and to give an update on his research assignments

Captain Norman Rechtman stops by to turn in scans of the previous commemorative book

Firefighter / photographer Jeff Vidal adds captions to pictures that will be used in the commemorative book

The Yearbook Committee would like to thank the following individuals for their contributions without which this book could not have been published.

Rich Brito

Mike Cardillo

Louis Carman

Steve Ciorrocco

Russ Chard

Hutch Clark

Dawn Clarke

Mark Claxon

Dan Dapolito

Lamar Davis

Don Dowell

Mark Ellis

Frank Emiliano

Ted Ferschke

Dan Fitzgerald

Eric Guerrero

Bill Gutierrez

Pat Hall

Marlene Harden

Rob Hazen

Jim Johnson

Mike Maalouf

Jack McMillan

Abby Montes

Hank Olmetti

Bernie Pflum

Matt Phillips

Dan Pittard

Dick Russell

Bill Sabino

Gary Smith

Christophe St. Luce

Joe Stolarz

Chris Sullivan

Dave Swick

Chris Taylor

Brian White

Ron White

Jim Ward

Rick Whippy

Hollywood Professional Firefighters Local #1375

Above: Victor Monette, Mike Cardillo and Bill Major enjoy a guided airboat ride in the Everglades. **At right:** the 2006 Firefighter Olympics Flag Football Team. (Top row) Eric Guerrero, Bobby Sterner, Pat Moore, Bill Huddleston, Jim Cummins, Brian Wilkie, Tom Price, Chris Sullivan. (Bottom row) Javier Carvajal, Dave Duensing, Matt Milone, Kenci Santil, and Pat Wilkie. **Below left:** Gary Peebles, Bob Allen, Frank Emiliano, Chuck Johnson, Steve Ciorrocco, Lamar Davis, Dave Swick, Dean Kelley, Jack McMillan, John Keelan, and Scott Bazy celebrate 25 years of service with the Department. **Below right:** Dave Swick and Carl Dempsey at the annual fishing tournament.

Above left: Allen Burchardt, Paul Watson, Gary Ethridge, and Rick Arndt catch up with each other. **Middle left:** Charles Colson, Holly Schmorr, and Peter Robinson having fun at T.Y. Park. **Bottom left:** Larry Allwine, Lamar Davis and Kevin Dodds. **Top right:** Bill Major and Don Dowell have something in common, "YabaDabaDo!" **Above:** Nice socks, Marty!

Top: *Norman Mahalsky and Marle Harden wish each other a Merry Christm.* **Middle left:** *Willie Conner, the barbec king.* **Middle right:** *Charlie Warner a. Charles Colson, twins?* **Bottom left:** *F Chief Virgil Fernandez in the make chair before a T.V. appearance — "I ready for my close-up, Mr. DeMill.* **Bottom right:** *Pete Hanna makes it ba to land, safely.*

Chief Fernandez serves as Armando Sanchez dishes it up

Kevin Dodds and Eric Guerrero working the grill at T.Y. Park while Dick Russell "supervises"

Top left: *Gary Sexsmith, "Happy St. Patty's, lad!"* **Bottom left:** *Gary Lehmann getting an earful from Joel Medina.* **Top right:** *Larry Allwine comes in first as "The King" at the talent show.* **Middle right:** *Beach Safety's Mark Mullen goes for first place at the City's first talent show.* **Bottom right:** *Jeff Davidson, Bob Aspinall, Chuck Colson, Larry Allwine, and Pete Robinson make time to support a worthy cause.*

Lori Marchetti, Janet Washburn, Rocio Cervini, Amy Schwarz, Marlene Harden and Dawn Clarke meet up at the Union Christmas Party

Mark Fritz, John Kusuk, Marc Croteau, Ken Cressler, Curtis Grier, Ron White, Alan Wasserman, Mark Claxon, and Eric Guerrero mug it up for the camera

A

Addicott, Claud 114
Allen, Christopher 74
Allen, Robert "Bob" 53, 141, 160
Allwine, Lawrence "Larry" 23, 24, 105, 113, 120, 135, 161, 164
Amy, Joseph "Joe" 74, 103, 107, 128
Anderson, Cathleen 4
Anderson, Don 107, 144, 146, 148, 149
Anderson, Judi 21, 22
App, Adam 74
Arndt, Robert "Rick" 65, 121, 161
Aspinall, Robert "Bob" 20, 43, 45, 85, 120, 129, 130, 131, 133, 138, 143, 164
Asseff, Patty 4
Austin, David 57, 63
Avilez, Derek 74, 106, 129

B

Bain, Keenan 69
Barbera, Charles "Charlie" 20, 23, 119, 124, 131
Barfield, Donald "Don" 54, 146, 148
Barnes, Wayne 148
Barnett, Richard 63
Barr, William 53
Battaglia, Walter 146, 148
Bazy, Robert "Scott" 3, 63, 90, 127, 157, 158, 160
Bealmear, Jack "Harry" 69, 85, 127
Beech, Alan 37, 40
Bell, Bill 147
Benson, Cameron 4, 5, 24
Biglin, William "Bill" 69, 103, 107, 122, 155
Blattner, Richard 4, 5
Blouin, Lisa 21, 22, 128, 132
Blundy, Daniel "Dan" 26, 27, 133
Bober, Peter 4
Bolivar, Jose 37, 40
Bouck, Charlie 148
Bouloy, Tanya 21, 143, 152, 157
Boyett, Kerry 74, 118, 124
Boyle, Chris 88
Bridenburg, John 63, 123, 151
Briosi, Michael "Mike" 66, 101, 140
Brito, James 74
Brito, Rich 141, 147, 148, 150, 159
Brown, Dick 141
Brown, Douglas 55
Bruce, Wayne 55, 120, 133
Bryan, Jay 63
Buckner, Bob 138
Burchardt, Allen "Al" 66, 127, 131, 161

Burgoon, C.E. 8, 11
Burke, Tim 48
Burns, George 48, 74, 101, 102, 106
Burrough, Randall "Randy" 9, 138, 140, 141, 148, 149
Busenbarrick, Beverly 21, 130, 149
Busenbarrick, Eric 43, 47, 142, 145
Butler, Mark 147

C

Cambra, Jill 37
Canosa, Vincent "Vince" 36, 118
Cardillo, Mike 116, 131, 155, 159, 160
Carman, Louis "Lou" 63, 119, 145, 159
Carpenter, David 37
Carvajal, Javier 160
Castano, Jorge 28, 29, 30, 117, 123
Cervini, Rocio 74, 106, 130, 165
Channer, Kevin 38
Chard, Russell "Russ" 66, 142, 145, 146, 154, 159
Cioppa, Anthony 74
Ciorrocco, Stephen "Steve" 57, 75, 140, 159, 160
Civita, David "Dave" 69, 122, 126
Clark, Hutch 148, 149, 159
Clark, William "Bill" 12, 148, 152
Clarke, Dawn 29, 75, 111, 121, 135, 159, 165
Claxon, Mark 17, 63, 108, 140, 159, 165
Clinton, Christopher "Chris" 75, 127
Cochran, Loran "Corky" 18, 53, 112, 153
Colebrooke, Rodney 23, 24
Colson, Charles "Chuck" 63, 123, 124, 129, 161, 162, 164
Comeau, Paul 141, 148
Conner, Donna 148, 149
Conner, William "Bill" 144, 148, 149, 156, 162
Cook, Holloway Lee 8, 11, 13, 91, 147
Cooke, Brian 66, 156
Cooper, Ed 17
Cooper, Martin "Marty" 20, 62, 114
Coughlin, Thomas 66
Cowart, Mark 69, 127
Coxe, Christopher "Chris" 48, 75
Coyne, John 8, 9, 16, 146, 147
Cressler, Kenneth "Ken" 69, 100, 138, 165
Croghan, Patrick 63
Cross, Andrea 38, 104
Cross, Michael 25
Croteau, Marc 66, 105, 108, 165

Csendes, Istvan 38
Cummins, James "Jim" 66, 117, 160
Curtis, Ralph 148
Cuthbert, Steve 146

D

D'Angelo, Donna 44, 45, 132
Damiano, Dan 148
Daniels, James 66
Danko, David "Dave" 20, 62, 103, 108, 116, 118, 143
Dapolito, Daniel "Dan" 70, 103, 124, 159
Davidson, Jeffrey "Jeff" 20, 62, 124, 143, 164
Davis, Andrew 70
Davis, Lamar 20, 22, 26, 27, 100, 113, 129, 132, 134, 137, 159, 160, 161
Davis, Leon 146
Davis, Shane 75
DeAbreu, Diana 55, 70, 102, 113, 123, 125, 127, 143, 145, 157
Delbert, Kenneth 64, 104
Delcampo, Chris 70
Dellerson, Richard 15, 27, 132
Dempsey, Carl 160
Desimone, Louis 38
Diah, Max 23
Dinges, Thomas 55, 64
Dingus, Tom 121
Dodds, Kevin 48, 75, 120, 124, 128, 136, 161, 163
Dollinger, Tom 38
Doret, Sidney 75
Dowell, Donald "Don" 110, 128, 133, 141, 142, 148, 149, 159, 161
Dowell, Kathy 148, 149
Downs, Jack 132, 148
Downs, Judy 132
Duensing, David "Dave" 75, 145, 160
Dunlap, Jac 141, 142

E

Edelman, Phillip "Phil" 75, 121, 124, 127, 128, 152
Ellis, Mark 66, 116, 159
Emiliano, Frank 70, 159, 160
Epstein, Jeff 38
Estevez, Andrew 76, 123
Ethridge, Gary 64, 147, 161
Ettinger, Brian 76, 143
Eutsey, Joseph "Joe" 3, 76, 90
Evans, Ernest 14
Eyerman, Dean 76, 101, 102, 113, 156

F

Falk, Peter "Pete" 76, 151

Fee, Mark 76
Ferguson, Bryan 38
Fernandez, Humberto "Bert" 76, 107, 122
Fernandez, Jose 76, 106
Fernandez, Virgil 6, 7, 9, 20, 22, 40, 59, 105, 126, 128, 129, 142, 143, 144, 147, 149, 162, 163
Ferschke, Pauline 149
Ferschke, Ted 148, 149, 152, 159
Fidler, Neil 17, 54
Fiorillo, Richard "Rick" 38, 112
Fisher, Fred 148
Fisher, Joseph "Joe" 70, 101, 113, 124
Fitzgerald, Courtney 152
Fitzgerald, Daniel "Dan" 53, 64, 104, 121, 142, 159
Fontaine, Frank 14
Ford, Gerald 14
Fox, George 15
Frattini, Evo 12
Fresco, Marcus 70, 117
Fritz, Mark 44, 46, 165
Frohock, Dave 148
Fuentes, Rafael 76
Fuentes, Ralph 100
Fulks, Michael "Mike" 67, 101, 108, 127
Furr, Beam 4

G

Gallo, Thomas "Tom" 25, 52
Gambino, Joseph "Joe" 20, 54, 56, 101, 109, 118, 123, 124, 129, 139, 143
Garcia, Analdy 77
Garcia, Jenny 38
Garcia, Juan 38
Garcia, Roberto 77
Geisler, George 140, 146, 148, 150
Gerkin, John 8
Giesler, George 110
Gilbert, Albert "Al" 53, 146
Giulianti, Mara 4
Gomez, Ernesto 38
Gonzalez, Leonardo 38
Gonzalez, Rodolfo 38
Graves, Kim 44, 45, 132
Greenfield, Barbara 132
Grier, Curtis 77, 165
Guernsey, David "Dave" 30, 48, 77, 118, 122, 141
Guerrero, Eric 70, 123, 132, 156, 159, 160, 163, 165
Guillod, Ed 147
Gulla, Michael "Mike" 35, 77, 106
Gurdyal, Janet 23, 132

Nelson, Andrew 80
Nerey, Belkys 127
Newmark, Stephen "Steve" 17, 54, 72, 111, 124

O

O'Brien, Joyce 39
O'Campo, Diego 39
O'Donnell, Hugh "Mike" 80, 129
O'Sheehan, Heidi 5
O'Toole, Dennis 55, 80
Oliveri, Sal 4
Olmetti, Henry "Hank" 80, 110, 125, 159
Ormston, Robert 39
Ornawka, Lucile 150

P

Palacio, Sergio 39
Park, Thomas "Tom" 16, 151
Parma, Ganga 25
Payne, Mark 72
Peebles, Gary 17, 54, 115, 141, 144, 160
Pender, Shana 81, 135
Perdue, Donald "Don" 53, 110
Pereira, Rita 48, 81
Perrin, Edward 39
Pflum, Bernard "Bernie" 72, 159
Phillips, Matthew "Matt" 44, 45, 54, 103, 159
Pichardo, Raymond 39
Pingol, Richard "Rick" 68, 143
Pittard, Dan 125, 138, 152, 159
Pittard, Daniel 81
Plummer, Christopher 81
Podger, William 15
Poli, Alexander "Alex" 42, 68, 127
Polistina, Sal 39
Politte, Kevin 68, 122
Poole, Tim 81
Powers, Raymond "Ray" 65, 129, 130
Prachtakov, Petko 39
Pratt, Christopher "Chris" 65, 101, 147
Preece, John 148
Price, Thomas "Tom" 72, 120, 121, 160
Puskarcik, Carl 39

Q

Quinn, Kevin 81, 151

R

Race, Edward 9, 12, 16
Ragusa, Rick 48
Ramos, Judi 23, 24
Ramsay, Mark 72, 101
Ray, Jerrel II 81
Reardon, Kevin 68, 117
Rechtman, Norman 65, 157, 158
Redding, Charles "Charlie" 72, 101, 126
Reekie, Kevin 81, 123
Reese, Steve "Wayne" 72, 128
Reilly, Peter 72
Renn, Ralph 148
Restrepo, Juan 52
Richards, Daryel 82, 152
Richards, James 152
Rienhart, Travis 81
Rieschl, Jon 82
Robertson, Garland 21, 24, 130
Robinson, Peter "Pete" 23, 24, 55, 114, 161, 164
Robledo, Eddie 39
Rohan, Joseph "Joe" 20, 22, 109, 110, 124, 129, 130, 131
Romano, Jeane 27

Gutierrez, William "Bill" 110, 118, 156, 159

H

Hall, Patricia "Pat" 130, 147, 150, 159
Hanna, Pete 114, 144, 148, 162
Hapsas, Michael 77
Harden, Marlene 77, 132, 159, 162, 165
Harvey, Richard "Rick" 77, 101, 108, 115
Havens, Jay 44, 47
Hay, Bobby 141
Hazen, Robert "Rob" 44, 45, 88, 119, 120, 159
Healey, Philip 67
Hegedus, Geza 30, 77, 102, 108
Helfen, Herbert "Herb" 24, 70, 120, 121
Hendrick, Patrick 37, 40, 42, 52
Hernandez, Javier 78, 107, 122, 127
Hershey, R.N. 8, 11
Hicks, John 67
Higgins, Gilbert 11, 153
Hodos, Martin "Marty" 12, 148
Hofacker, Joyce 150
Hofle, Marcy 127
Hogue, Bonnie 26, 27, 132
Holden, Hoyt 18
Holden, Lloyd 141
Holland, Jay 11
Holm, Michael 71
Holoubek, Rodger 21, 22, 24, 130
Holtfreter, Andrew 78
Huddleston, William "Bill" 147, 151, 160
Hughes, Nathan "Nate" 78, 143
Hyde, Ted 78, 130

I

sbill, Charlie 141

J

ames, Desiree 141
ames, Lonnie 14
ames, Morris 20, 62, 101, 110, 124, 141, 143, 152, 157
clev, Mario 38
ohnson, Charles "Chuck" 71, 116, 118, 160
ohnson, Connie 149

Johnson, Jim 134, 148, 149, 159
Johnson, John 64, 116
Jones, James "Steve" 64, 156
Jones, William "Bill" 60, 71, 101, 139
Jordan, Daniel "Dan" 78, 107, 118
Jurado, Rodolfo "Rudy" 67, 123

K

Karl, Thomas "Tom" 53, 101, 106, 125, 134, 144, 148
Kay, Bill 119
Kebler, John 67, 85, 100
Keelan, John 17, 78, 160
Keller, Patrick 67
Kellerman, John 16, 53, 67, 132
Kelley, Hal "Dean" 71, 160
Kimmich, Bob 141
Klitch, Bill 144
Knott, David "Dave" 71, 107, 119
Korn, Christofer "Chris" 67, 125
Kuchenberg, Rudy 85, 120, 141
Kuklinski, John 64, 117, 127, 145
Kuklinski, John 64, 117, 127, 145
Kusuk, John 67, 113, 114, 140, 165

L

Ladwig, Robert "Kurt" 68, 107, 123, 127
Lana, Juan 71, 123, 1126, 129
Lanciault, Guy 17, 64, 107
Lassiter, Donald 71
Latore, Lawrence "Larry" 55, 116, 127
Laucella, Cathy 37
Lehmann, Gary 42, 78, 114, 164
Lenox, Charlie 146
Li, Mitchell 48, 78
Liddell, Anthony "Tony" 55, 78, 129
Lorenzo, Herminio 9, 134, 149
Lucas, Kaley 38, 41
Lunsford, Fred 148
Luongo, Steve 17, 144
Lynch, Francis 38

M

Maalouf, Michael "Mike" 79, 159
MacKinlay, Kevin 39
Macko, Nick 40, 41
Macready, Douglas "Doug" 16, 17, 146
Madge, Robert "Bob" 54, 118, 141
Mahalsky, Norman 138, 162
Mailliard, Wayne 53

Major, William "Bill" 19, 60, 64, 125, 160, 161
Malavsky, Morton 17
Malliard, Wayne 110, 135
Manion, Larry 141
Manion, Mel 152
Manos, John 59, 79, 122
Mansker, Cindy 17
Marchetti, Lori 79, 106, 111, 165
Marold, James 79
Marrero, Fernando 39, 40, 111
Martin, Steven 71
Martinez, Daniel "Dan" 71, 145
Matthews, William 18
McAdams, Gabby 39
McCall, George 153
McCann, Mark 79, 121, 129
McCarry, Daniel "Dan" 79, 101, 131
McGillivray, Sean 68
McManus, Michael 37
McMillan, John "Jack" 54, 133, 144, 156, 159, 160
Meadows, Art 152
Medina, Garrett 152
Medina, Joel 28, 29, 30, 152, 164
Mello, Joseph 13, 15
Mendia, Jose 79, 131
Mertes, Amy 79
Meyer, Frank 113, 117, 156
Mikell, Thomas 53
Miller, Mark 68, 121, 128, 135
Milone, Matthew "Matt" 79116, 160
Miranda, Kenneth "Ken" 80, 121, 128
Monette, Victor 72, 160
Montes, Abiud "Abi" 60, 80, 108, 132, 159
Montgomery, Robert "Bob" 61, 80, 101, 121
Moore, Mack 44, 45
Moore, Patrick "Pat" 68, 129, 152, 160
Morales, Jose 48, 55, 65
Moran, Edward 9, 17, 53
Mossop, Andrew "Drew" 80, 106
Mott, James "Ron" 80, 115, 130, 140
Mullen, Mark 37, 164
Muniz, Tony 88
Munson, Robert "Bob" 65, 110
Muscarella, Joe 147, 148

N

Nagel, Eugene 26

Rose, Dale 28
Rose, Klaus 82
Rudasill, Dennis 65
Russell, Dick 144, 148, 150, 159, 163
Russo, Frances 4
Russo, James "Jim" 82, 110, 152

S

Sabino, Bill 148, 159
Saffran, Michael 82
Saffran, Sandra 21
Salerno, Dave 150
Salerno, Jeff 150
Sanchez, Armando 82, 143, 163
Santil, Kenci 160
Saredy, John 68
Saunders, Jack 58, 82, 120
Savery, Bill 141, 148, 152
Schmorr, Holly 82, 121, 138, 157, 161
Schwarz, Amy 82, 115, 143, 165
Seamanson, Kent 109
Selby, David 69, 123
Serrao, Simon 83
Sexsmith, Gary 43, 46, 117, 137, 164
Sheldon, David "Dave" 73, 107
Shelton, John 54, 69, 110
Sherwood, Linda 5
Shoemaker, James "Jim" 36, 40, 41, 112
Shulby, Ronald 53
Simione, Jason 83, 101, 113
Skinner, Gary 107, 139
Smith, Gary 23, 54, 123, 126, 129, 137, 159

St. Luce, Christophe 159
Steele, Mark 20, 28, 30, 113, 121, 123, 124, 129, 133
Steinbuck, Henry 83, 128, 131
Sterner, Bobby 160
Stolarz, Joseph "Joe" 65, 159
Sullivan, Christopher "Chris" 29, 83, 106, 118, 122, 129, 152, 159, 160
Swick, David "Dave" 65, 159, 160

T

Taffel, Cindy 83
Tarmey, Ed 141
Taylor, Joseph 37, 42
Taylor, Richard "Chris" 60, 83, 113, 116, 135, 159
Thomas, Sherrick 14
Thomas, Susan "Sue" 18, 59, 73
Thompson, Pete 39
Toncos, Jim 113, 141, 142, 148
Treadwell, Marcy 59, 83, 122, 135
Tullio, Charles "Chuck" 73, 123, 145
Turner, James 39
Tursi, Richard 73

U

Ura, Adam 83, 127

V

Velez, Pablo 39
Venezia, Christopher 73
Vera, Anthony "Tony" 83, 111, 129
Vezi, Mark 40
Vidal, Jeffrey "Jeff" 84, 124, 157, 158

Vinas, Anthony "Tony" 84, 132

W

Wade, Frank 17, 73, 110, 111, 151
Wadlow, James 40, 41, 42
Wagner, Raymond "Ray" 42, 84, 106
Ward, Jim 9, 16, 140, 141, 148, 149, 150, 159
Ward, Kathy 148
Warner, Charlie 162
Warren, George 15, 28
Washburn, Janet 44, 47, 123, 132, 165
Wasserman, Alan "Al" 73, 129, 165
Watson, Paul 73, 103, 161
Webb, Jeffrey 84
Wells, Josh 48, 84
Wenth, John 119
Whippy, Peggy 148, 150
Whippy, Rick 114, 141, 148, 150, 159
White, Brian 54, 73, 101, 106, 115, 124, 136, 159
White, Ronald "Ron" 69, 106, 129, 136, 159, 165
White, Roy "Skip" 44, 45, 116
Wilkie, A.J. 8, 11
Wilkie, Brian 84, 101, 160
Wilkie, Bruce 40, 41
Wilkie, Patrick "Pat" 84, 106, 123, 160
Williams, John 16
Wilson, Jack 148
Wittkamp, A.M. 8, 11
Woodruff, James F. 11, 153
Woodward, Christine 21

Wright, Jim 148

Y

Yost, Leo 40
Young, Joseph 11, 14, 18

Z

Zelenka, Steven 106
Ziadie, Jameel 84
Zinkil, Bill 147

9 781681 621937